Essential GCSE
Latin

Essential GCSE Latin

Second Edition

John Taylor

Bloomsbury Academic
An imprint of Bloomsbury Publishing Plc

B L O O M S B U R Y
LONDON · OXFORD · NEW YORK · NEW DELHI · SYDNEY

Bloomsbury Academic
An imprint of Bloomsbury Publishing Plc

50 Bedford Square	1385 Broadway
London	New York
WC1B 3DP	NY 10018
UK	USA

www.bloomsbury.com

BLOOMSBURY and the Diana logo are trademarks of Bloomsbury Publishing Plc

First published 2014
Reprinted by Bloomsbury Academic 2015 (three times)

British Library Cataloguing-in-Publication Data
A catalogue record for this book is available from the British Library.

ISBN: PB: 978-1-4725-1011-2
ePUB: 978-1-4725-0677-1
ePDF: 978-1-4725-1472-1

Library of Congress Cataloging-in-Publication Data
A catalog record for this book is available from the Library of Congress.

Typeset by RefineCatch, Bungay, Suffolk
Printed and bound in India

CONTENTS

Preface   viii
Abbreviations   x
Glossary of grammar terms   xii
The importance of word endings   xvi

Nominative case   1
Vocative case   4
Accusative case   5
Genitive case   7
Dative case   9
Ablative case   10
Declension and gender   12
First declension nouns   13
Second declension nouns   15
Third declension nouns   18
Fourth and fifth declension nouns   22
Adjectives   24
Agreement of nouns and adjectives   27
Comparative adjectives   29
Superlative adjectives   31
Irregular comparative and superlative adjectives   33
Adverbs   35
Comparative and superlative adverbs   38
Pronouns   40
Personal pronouns   41
Possessives   45
This and *that*   48
Self and *same*   51
Relative pronoun (*who, which*) and clause   54
Less common pronouns   57
Prepositions   61

Prefixes and compound verbs	64
Conjunctions	66
Verbs and conjugations	68
Present tense	70
Imperfect tense	71
Future tense	73
Infinitive	74
The verb *to be*	75
Principal parts	77
Perfect tense	78
Common irregular perfect tenses	80
Pluperfect tense	83
Very irregular verbs	85
Defective verbs	90
Active and passive	91
Present, imperfect and future passive	93
Agent and instrument	95
Perfect and pluperfect passive	96
Passive infinitive	98
Deponent verbs	99
Semi-deponent verbs	101
Direct commands	102
Direct questions	104
Numerals	107
Time expressions	109
Time clauses	111
Because and *although* clauses	113
If clauses (conditionals)	114
Connecting relative	116
Present active participle	118
Perfect passive participle	121
Common irregular perfect passive participles	123
Perfect active participle (from deponent verbs)	124
Future active participle	126
Disentangling participles	128
Ablative absolute	129
Indirect statement	132
Imperfect subjunctive	138
Purpose clauses	140

Other ways of expressing purpose   142
Indirect commands   144
Result clauses   146
Verbs of fearing   149
Pluperfect subjunctive   150
Cum clauses   152
Indirect questions   154
Negatives   157
Translating complex sentences   159
Important words with more than one meaning   162
Words easily confused   164
Summary of uses of the subjunctive   167

Appendix: Practice translation passages   169
Vocabulary   184
Index   199

PREFACE

This book (first published in 2006 and now presented in a revised second edition) is a summary of all the linguistic requirements for GCSE Latin (current OCR specification). It is neither a complete course from scratch nor a traditional reference grammar (though it could at a pinch be used as either). It is aimed mainly at pupils in their GCSE year, though I hope it may also have a use in other contexts where the threads of previous study need to be pulled together (for scholarship preparation, or after transfer to a new school or a new teacher). Whatever textbook pupils have used, many remain very hazy about grammar. It is difficult to track back in a multi-volume course to the first introduction of a particular construction. Traditional grammars on the other hand can be forbidding, and often do not give enough help with syntax and idiom. This book breaks everything down into bite-sized chunks, with examples and practice sentences (650 in all) on each point. There is some deliberate repetition, but much more use of cross-referencing. The treatment is not purely sequential: sentences testing nouns have to include verbs (and in particular the opening exercises on case usage anticipate much that follows), but complications irrelevant to the point under discussion have as far as possible been avoided. *Essential GCSE Latin* concentrates on the understanding of principles, both in the formation of words and in the construction of sentences, in order to reduce the need for rote learning. Every year examiners' reports comment that many candidates muddle through translation and comprehension passages with too little attention to grammar: endings are ignored, and common constructions not recognised. This book is an invitation to take grammar seriously and to understand its basic terminology. To keep things simple and save space, a default system operates in grammatical description: a verb is active unless specified as passive, indicative unless specified as subjunctive. The book uses the aggregate vocabulary of 475 words prescribed by OCR for the papers *Language 1* and *Language 2*; example sentences stick where practicable to the subset list for *Language 1*. The Appendix provides fifteen translation passages at the level of *Language 2*. Exercises in the style of both papers can be found in Henry Cullen, Michael Dormandy and John Taylor, *Latin Stories* (Bristol Classical Press 2011); see also Ashley Carter, *Latin Language Tests for Levels 1, 2 and GCSE* (Bristol Classical Press 2011). I have not made special provision for OCR Foundation Tier or for other qualifications (WJEC Certificates, IGCSE), but core vocabulary and grammar are relatively consistent and much of the book should be useful to candidates preparing for any of these examinations, as well as to older students beginning or returning to Latin.

I happily acknowledge a debt (particularly in the Glossary of grammar terms) to James Morwood, *A Latin Grammar* (Oxford University Press 1999), to which I refer any reader who considers my concentration on GCSE requirements to involve excessive economy with the truth. I am very grateful to Charlotte Loveridge at Bloomsbury for her help with this second edition, and I repeat my thanks to Deborah Blake and Ray Davies for their guidance of the first.

John Taylor
Tonbridge School

ABBREVIATIONS

abl	ablative
acc	accusative
adj	adjective
adv	adverb
conj	conjunction
dat	dative
dep	deponent
f	feminine
gen	genitive
imperat	imperative
indecl	indeclinable (does not change its endings)
irreg	irregular
lit	literally
m	masculine
n	neuter
nom	nominative
num	numeral
pl	plural
prep	preposition
pron	pronoun
refl	reflexive
s-dep	semi-deponent
sg	singular
sup	superlative

usu	usually
voc	vocative
1, 2, 3	first, second, third person; first, second, third etc. declension
1st, 2nd, 3rd	first, second, third etc. conjugation

Note also two abbreviations of Latin expressions which are common in English, and frequently used in the explanations of grammar in this book:

e.g.	*exempli gratia*	for (the sake of) example
i.e.	*id est*	that is (*introducing further explanation*)

GLOSSARY OF GRAMMAR TERMS

ablative	case expressing *by*, *with*, *from*; used with prepositions expressing motion away from, or being in a place.
accusative	case of direct object; used with prepositions expressing motion towards; used for subject of infinitive in indirect statement.
active	form of verb where the grammatical subject is the doer of the action (as distinct from passive).
adjective	word describing a noun (with which it agrees in number, gender and case).
adverb	word describing a verb (or an adjective, or another adverb).
agree	have the same number (agreement of subject and verb); have the same number, gender and case (agreement of noun and adjective).
ambiguous	can mean more than one thing.
antecedent	noun or pronoun in main clause to which relative pronoun refers back.
auxiliary	a verb (usually part of *to be*) used with a participle to form a tense of another verb (e.g. perfect passive *portati sumus* = we have been carried).
case	form of a noun, pronoun or adjective that shows the job it does in the sentence (e.g. accusative for direct object); cases are arranged in the order nominative, (vocative), accusative, genitive, dative, ablative.
clause	part of a sentence with its own subject and verb.
comparative	form of an adjective or adverb meaning *more*, *-er* (e.g. *longior* = longer).
complement	another nominative word or phrase describing the subject.
compound	verb with prefix (e.g. *exire* = to go out).
conditional	clause beginning *if* or *unless*.
conjugate	go through the different parts of a verb (e.g. *porto, portas, portat* etc).
conjugation	one of the four main patterns by which verbs change their endings.
conjunction	word joining clauses, phrases or words together (e.g. *and, but, therefore*).

consonant	letter representing a sound that can only be used together with a vowel.
construction	pattern according to which a particular type of sentence or clause (e.g. indirect statement) is formed.
dative	case of indirect object, often translated *to* or *for.*
declension	one of the patterns (three main ones, also used for adjectives, and two less common) by which nouns change their endings.
decline	go through the different parts of a noun, pronoun or adjective in case order.
deponent	verb that is passive in form but active in meaning.
defective verb	verb of which only a few parts exist.
direct object	noun or pronoun on the receiving end of action of verb.
direct speech	actual words of a speaker, usually enclosed by inverted commas.
ending	last bit of a word, added to the stem to give more information and show its job in the sentence.
feminine	one of the three genders, for females or things imagined as female.
finite	form of a verb with tense and person ending (as distinct from infinitive or participle).
future	tense of verb referring to something that will happen in the future.
gender	one of three categories (masculine, feminine, neuter) into which nouns and pronouns are put according to their actual or imagined sex or lack of it.
genitive	case expressing possession or definition, often translated *of.*
gerundive	adjective formed from verb, expressing the idea *needing to be done*; used with *ad* to express purpose.
homonym	word coincidentally spelled in the same way as another unrelated word.
imperative	form of verb used for direct command.
imperfect	tense of verb referring to incomplete, extended or repeated action in the past.
indeclinable	does not change its endings.
indicative	form of verb expressing a fact (usually as distinct from subjunctive).
indirect	indirect statement, command or question is the reported form of it (as distinct from quotation of the speaker's actual words); indirect object is person or thing in the dative indirectly affected by action of verb, e.g. *I gave the money* (direct object) *to the old man* (indirect object).
infinitive	form of verb introduced by *to*, expressing the basic meaning (e.g. *currere* = to run).

intransitive	verb that does not have a direct object (e.g. *festino* = I hurry).
irregular	word that does not follow one of the standard declensions or conjugations.
literally	translated in a way corresponding closely to the Latin words, but which needs to be modified to produce natural English.
locative	special case ending of some nouns expressing *at* or *in*.
main clause	clause that makes sense on its own, and expresses the main point of a sentence (as distinct from subordinate clause).
masculine	one of the three genders, for males or things imagined as male.
negative	expressing that something is not the case or should not happen.
neuter	one of the three genders, for things imagined as neither male nor female.
nominative	case used for subject of sentence.
noun	word naming a person or thing (e.g. *urbs* = city; a *proper* noun with a capital letter gives its actual name e.g. *Roma* = Rome).
number	being either singular or plural.
numerals	numbers.
object	noun or pronoun acted upon by a verb.
part of speech	category of word (noun, adjective, pronoun, verb, adverb, preposition, conjunction).
participle	adjective formed from a verb (e.g. *portans* = carrying, *portatus* = having been carried).
passive	form of verb where the subject does not do the action but is on the receiving end of it (e.g. *capior* = I am captured).
perfect	tense of verb referring to a completed action in the past.
person	term for the subject of verb: first person = *I, we*; second person = *you*, third person = *he, she, it, they* (or a noun replacing one of these).
phrase	group of words not containing a finite verb (as distinct from clause).
pluperfect	tense of verb referring to something that had already happened by a particular point in the past.
plural	more than one.
possessive	adjective or pronoun expressing who or what something belongs to.
prefix	word or syllable added to the beginning of another word.
preposition	word used with a noun or pronoun in the accusative or ablative to focus more closely the meaning of the case (e.g. *into*).

present	tense of a verb referring to something that is happening now (or, in the case of a present participle, at the same time as the action described by main verb of the sentence).
principal parts	set of (usually four) parts of a verb from which you can work out all necessary information about it: present tense (first person singular), infinitive, perfect tense (first person singular), perfect passive participle (if the verb has one).
pronoun	word that stands instead of a noun, avoiding the need to repeat it.
reflexive	word referring back to the subject of the verb.
relative	subordinate clause (or pronoun introducing it) relating to person or thing just mentioned in the main clause.
sentence	group of words with subject and verb (and often other elements) that can stand on its own (as distinct from phrase or subordinate clause).
singular	just one (as distinct from plural).
stem	the part of a word that stays the same: different endings are added to give more information and show the job it does in the sentence.
subject	noun or pronoun in the nominative case, expressing who or what does the action (with active verb) or is on the receiving end of it (with passive verb).
subjunctive	form of verb referring not to a fact but to an idea or possibility (as distinct from indicative).
subordinate	of secondary importance to something else; a subordinate clause cannot stand alone but only makes sense in relation to the main clause.
superlative	form of adjective or adverb meaning *very, most, -est* (e.g. *altissimus* = very high, highest).
supply	provide in translation a word that is not separately represented in Latin but worked out from the grammar and context (e.g. *multa dixit* = he said many *things*).
syllable	part of a word forming a spoken unit, usually consisting of vowel with consonants before or after or both.
tense	form of a verb showing when the action takes place (in the past, present or future).
transitive	verb that has a direct object.
verb	word expressing an action.
vocative	case used for addressing someone or something.
vowel	letter representing a sound that can be spoken by itself: *a, e, i, o, u, y.*

THE IMPORTANCE OF WORD ENDINGS

English depends mainly on word order to show what job each word does in a sentence. A simple sentence has the order *subject, verb, object*:

> The boy is looking for the girl.

Latin behaves in a different way. There are indeed some typical patterns (though they are different from English), so that a simple sentence often has the order *subject, object, verb*:

> puer puellam quaerit.
> The boy is looking for the girl.

But this is much less important than the word endings. If the word endings and the word order seem to be in conflict, the endings win every time:

> puellam puer quaerit.
>
> *still means* The boy is looking for the girl.

If you ask why put it in this peculiar order, the answer is for emphasis, to give special stress (in this example) to the accusative word that has been hauled to the front of the sentence:

> The boy is looking for *the girl* (*implying* and not someone else).
>
> *or* It is the girl the boy is looking for.

In this second translation the grammar of the Latin is modified but the word order is preserved. You can only reverse the *meaning* by swapping the case endings:

> puella puerum quaerit.
> The girl is looking for the boy.

A recent GCSE unseen translation passage included the following sentence (in direct speech, as an announcement to the crowded Forum in Rome):

proelio magno victi sumus.

The heading explained that the story was about the Romans' disastrous defeat in battle by the Carthaginian general, Hannibal, at Lake Trasimene in 217 BC. Despite this, and despite the grammar, a large number of candidates wrote something like: *We have won a big battle*. This shows the hazards of simply taking the basic meaning of the words, then trying to create a sentence out of them. Just like failing to apply common sense in squaring the heading with the story, ignoring endings is *failing to use information you have been given*: this accounts for more lost marks in GCSE than anything else. Basic knowledge of endings should have enabled all candidates to spot that *proelio magno* must be dative or ablative (in fact it is ablative), and that *victi sumus* is perfect passive. The correct translation is of course:

We have been defeated in a big battle.

That is what to write for full marks. Note however that the Latin sentence gets its impact from the progressive way in which the news is revealed. Imagine we are Romans in the listening crowd: *proelio* tells us there has been a battle, *magno* that it was a big one, *victi* that some people have been defeated, and *sumus* that those people are us. Because the endings give the basic meaning, the word order is freed up to create other effects. Word endings are neither an optional extra nor a necessary nuisance but the essential means of understanding Latin properly, enjoying it and getting good results. This book aims to help you to use efficiently the information that endings provide.

NOMINATIVE CASE

A *case* is the form a noun, pronoun or adjective takes to show the job it does in the sentence. Its name comes from *casus* (= a falling): like *a bad case of measles* (the way events fall out), but not *a good case of wine* (that is a *homonym*). In Latin grammar the other cases are imagined as falling away at increasing angles from the upright purity of the nominative. This also explains the terms *decline* and *declension*: in listing the cases of a particular word in order, you trace the pattern by which they fall away from the vertical.

- Refer to the Glossary (pages xii–xv) for any grammar terms not fully understood.

The nominative is used for the subject of a sentence or clause. The term comes from *nomen*, stem *nomin-* (= name): the nominative *names* the person or thing the sentence is going to be about. In a typical sentence with an active verb, it refers to the person who does the action:

servus murum aedificat.
The slave builds the wall.

Regular nominative endings for the three main declensions:

	first	second	third
sg	-a	-us (-um *if n*)	(*wide range of possibilities*)
pl	-ae	-i (-a *if n*)	-es (-a *if n*)

- See full tables of noun declensions: pages 13–23.

A singular subject must have a singular verb: noun and verb must *agree* in number. Two singulars make a plural:

puer et puella per viam ambulabant.
The boy and the girl were walking along the street.

A nominative word very frequently begins a sentence. If a sentence does not start with a nominative, the subject of the verb usually has to be worked out from the verb ending:

clamorem audivimus.
We heard a shout.

The verb can tell you if the subject is third person, but cannot by itself tell you who it refers to. When a third person verb has no subject expressed, you normally assume the subject is the same as that of the previous sentence:

> servus cibum abstulit. deinde e villa fugit.
> The slave stole the food. Then he fled from the house.

Less commonly, a nominative word may be in the sentence, but postponed in order to put another word first for emphasis (first and last in the sentence are the strongest positions for this purpose):

> cibum servus abstulit, non pecuniam.
> The slave stole *food* (*or* It was *food* the slave stole), not *money*.

Another noun or descriptive phrase referring to the subject is also nominative:

> miles, vir ingens, ianuam facile rupit.
> The soldier, a huge man, easily broke the door.

A second nominative also follows the verb *to be*:

> frater meus nauta est.
> My brother is a sailor.

The second noun here is called the *complement*. Contrast this with the accusative object:

> frater meus nautam salutavit.
> My brother greeted the sailor.

The nominative is quoted as the basic form of a noun (or adjective or pronoun), but it is not simply a default case. A word can only be nominative if it is the subject of a *finite* verb, i.e. a verb with a tense and a person ending. Any sentence contains or implies a nominative as the subject of the main verb. A complex sentence can include one or more *additional* nominatives (each the subject of a subordinate clause) if it meets this requirement:

> cum amici advenissent, pueri adeo riserunt ut senex iratus esset.
> When <u>their friends</u> had arrived, <u>the boys</u> laughed so much that <u>the old man</u> was angry.

This rule explains why in an indirect statement the subject of the infinitive is accusative (see page 132). In general a Latin word that does not qualify as nominative is most likely to be accusative or ablative (see pages 129–31 on ablative absolute).

Note that all proper names in a passage (usually given underneath, with grammar details) need to be *put back into the nominative* in translation:

omnes Caesarem salutavimus.
We all greeted Caesar.

VOCATIVE CASE

This is used to address or speak directly to someone. Its name comes from *voco* (= I call). Older books list it separately after the nominative when they set out noun declensions, making six cases rather than five. It is now normally just shown as a footnote where necessary: the vocative is the same as the nominative for most singulars and all plurals (and applies only to nouns and adjectives, not pronouns).

The main distinctive vocative form to note is the ending *-e* for second declension masculine nouns (see page 15):

sg	nom	domin-us
	voc	domin-e

- Note that *filius* (= son) drops the *-e*, so that its vocative is *fili*.

A vocative is usually easy to spot in a sentence. It is often separated off by a comma or commas. It is often found together with an imperative (see page 102). It is even easier to recognise when preceded by *o* (as a dignified form of address, e.g. in prayers), though this is usually better omitted in English.

cenam mihi para, serve.
Prepare dinner for me, slave!

audite nos, o deae.
Hear us, goddesses!

- For the *locative*, which has no connection with the vocative but is another (and much rarer) case additional to those usually listed, see page 63.

ACCUSATIVE CASE

The accusative gets its name from *accuso* (= I accuse). That may not seem very informative, but it captures by one example the idea of *homing in on a target*: this is what the accusative does, in two main ways.

(1) It is used for the *direct object*, the person or thing on the receiving end of the action expressed by the verb:

> puer librum incendit.
> The boy burned the book.

(2) It is used, with or without a preposition (see below and page 61), to express *motion towards* (the destination being thought of as a target just as the direct object is):

> Romam profecti sumus.
> We set out for Rome.

Regular accusative endings for the three main declensions:

	first	*second*	*third*
sg	-am	-um	-em (*like nom if n*)
pl	-as	-os (-a *if n*)	-es (-a *if n*)

Note that the verbs *doceo* (= I teach) and *rogo* (= I ask) can take a double accusative:

> dominus servum nova verba docuit.
> The master taught the slave some new words.

This must be distinguished from a hidden indirect object, where one of the nouns is actually dative (see page 9):

> senex pecuniam servo dedit.
> The old man gave the slave the money (i.e. gave it *to* him).

The accusative is used with prepositions expressing motion towards or through (see page 61):

> ad Italiam navigavimus.
> We sailed towards Italy.

With the names of towns and cities (and islands small enough to count as one town) the preposition is omitted.

The idea of *motion through* also explains why the accusative is used for *time how long* (see page 109):

> multas horas in villa manebamus.
> We stayed in the house for many hours.

The accusative is used as *subject* of the infinitive in an indirect statement (see page 132):

> nuntius dixit turbam convenire.
> The messenger said that a crowd was gathering.

For the way to deal with a sentence whose first word is accusative, see pages 1–2.

GENITIVE CASE

The genitive gets its name from the adjective form of the Latin *genitus*, meaning *birth* or *origin* (compare *Genesis*). The underlying idea is the *source* from which something comes, but in practice the genitive normally expresses *possession* (things *belonging to* people being imagined as *originating from* them). It is translated *of*, or (often more naturally) represented by the use of an apostrophe (before *s* for a singular, after it for a plural):

> haec est villa senatoris.
> This is the house of the senator.
>
> *or* This is the senator's house.

	first	*second*	*third*
sg	-ae	-i	-is
pl	-arum	-orum	-(i)um

Regular genitive endings for the three main declensions:

As well as expressing possession, the genitive is used in many other places where English uses *of*. A genitive plural often follows a superlative (see page 31):

> optimus servorum adest.
> The best (one) of the slaves is here.

More generally, it often expresses *part* of a larger group or whole:

> multi civium discesserunt.
> Many of the citizens left.

> partem libri legi.
> I have read part of the book.

The word *plus* (= more) is treated as a noun meaning *a larger quantity*, and is always followed by a genitive:

> da mihi plus cibi.
> *literally* Give me more of food!
> *i.e.* Give me more food!

It is also possible to use *multum* (= much) and *nihil* (= nothing) with a genitive in a similar way:

> multum sanguinis vidimus.
> We saw much blood (*literally* much of blood).

> nihil gaudii accipio ubi talia audio.
> I get no pleasure (*literally* nothing of pleasure) when I hear such things.

Note that in these singular examples, the word *of* is omitted when translating the genitive.

DATIVE CASE

The dative case gets its name from *do* (= I give), perfect passive participle *datus*. Its basic idea is of *giving*: literally handing over something to someone, or doing something for them. It is usually translated *to* or *for*.

	first	*second*	*third*
	Regular dative endings for the three main declensions:		
sg	-ae	-o	-i
pl	-is	-is	-ibus

The dative is used for the *indirect object* of a sentence:

> cives senatori praemium dederunt.
> The citizens gave the senator a prize.

> puella cenam seni paravit.
> The girl prepared dinner for the old man.

In English, if the indirect object comes before the direct, *to* is often omitted (but if the indirect object comes second, *to* must be included):

> femina filio librum dedit.
> The woman gave her son a book.
> *or* The woman gave a book to her son.

Some verbs, because of their meaning, are followed by a dative instead of an accusative:

appropinquo	I approach	(I come near *to* something)
credo	I believe, I trust	(I give trust *to* someone)
faveo	I favour	(I give favour *to* someone)
impero	I order	(I give an order *to* someone)
persuadeo	I persuade	(I apply persuasion *to* someone)
resisto	I resist	(I put up resistance *to* someone)

ABLATIVE CASE

The ablative gets its name from *ablatus*, the perfect passive participle of *aufero* (= I carry away): so, *carried away*. As with the name of the accusative, this does not seem very informative, but it captures one important idea the ablative expresses: *separation* or going away. The ablative is a bit of a ragbag, but many of its meanings are covered by the translations *by, with* or *from*.

Regular ablative endings for the three main declensions:

	first	*second*	*third*
sg	-a	-o	-e (*often -i for adjectives*)
pl	-is	-is	-ibus

The ablative is used with prepositions meaning *going away from*, and also (less predictably) ones meaning *staying* in a place (see page 62):

omnes cives e foro festinaverunt.
All the citizens hurried out of the forum.

nemo in foro manebat.
No-one stayed in the forum.

With a passive verb the ablative is used both for the agent (the person *by whom* the action is done), with the preposition *a* (*ab* in front of a vowel or *h*), and for the instrument (the thing *with which* it is done), without a preposition (see page 95 for both):

rex ab uxore gladio necatus est.
The king was killed by his wife with a sword.

The ablative is used to express *time when*, and also *time within which* (see page 109):

amici nostri prima luce profecti paucis horis advenient.
Our friends, having set out at first light, will be here within a few hours.

A participle phrase not connected grammatically to the rest of the sentence is put in the ablative as an *ablative absolute* (see pages 129–31):

signo dato, milites urbem oppugnare coeperunt.
When the signal had been given, the soldiers began to attack the city.

The ablative can be used after a comparative, instead of an expression with *quam*, to mean *than* (see page 30):

hic puer fratre stultior est.
This boy is more stupid than his brother.

Exercise 1   Case usage (i)

 1 senex pecuniam nobis dedit.
 2 pater puellae in urbe habitat.
 3 omnes Romam festinavimus.
 4 frater meus miles est.
 5 dominus servis cenam paravit.
 6 milites clamoribus feminarum vocantur.
 7 hostes Romanorum in castra subito irruperunt.
 8 cives verbis regis non credebant.
 9 dux militum epistulam uxori misit.
10 statim responde mihi, serve!

Exercise 2   Case usage (ii)

 1 aquam nunc bibo, non vinum.
 2 canis in via multas horas iacebat.
 3 nauta, vir fortis, liberos e periculo servavit.
 4 o dei, quando auxilium nobis mittetis?
 5 senex pueros nova verba docuit.
 6 navis paucis diebus ad terram adveniet.
 7 mercator a servis nocte necatus est.
 8 multi civium consulem in foro exspectabant.
 9 pater sapientior est filio.
10 hoc libro lecto, omnia intellego.

DECLENSION AND GENDER

A declension is a *type* of noun (or adjective or pronoun), one of several fixed patterns according to which these words change their endings (for different cases, and for singular and plural). We do not have anything very close to this in English: only pronouns change case (for example *I* into *me*: see page 40), but note the different ways English nouns form their plurals:

most add *-s* (*book* and *books*) or *-es* (*bus* and *buses*)
a few add a different ending (*child* and *children*)
a few change a vowel (*man* and *men*)
a few stay the same (*sheep*)

Latin declensions are roughly comparable to this. In English the unusual plurals are just minor exceptions to one general rule, but in Latin there are three main patterns (plus two much less common ones).

Gender is the sex that a word has or is imagined to have. In French everything is either masculine or feminine. In English most inanimate objects are regarded as neuter (*it*), though, for example, a ship is thought of as feminine (. . . *all who sail in her*). Latin has a neuter gender, but still regards most objects as masculine or feminine.

Declension is not the same as gender, but there is some correlation between them. The vast majority of first declension nouns are feminine, but a few are masculine. Second declension nouns ending *-us* are the other way round: almost all are masculine. There are variant versions of the second and of the third declension for nouns that are neuter: with neuter nouns the accusative is always the same as the nominative, and the nominative and accusative plurals always end in *-a*.

A few nouns, e.g. *civis* (= citizen), can be either masculine or feminine according to context.

FIRST DECLENSION NOUNS

Pattern of endings:			
sg	*nom*	-a	
	acc	-am	
	gen	-ae	
	dat	-ae	
	abl	-a	
pl	*nom*	-ae	
	acc	-as	
	gen	-arum	
	dat	-is	
	abl	-is	

		girl	
		f	
sg	*nom*	puell-a	
	acc	puell-am	
	gen	puell-ae	
	dat	puell-ae	
	abl	puell-a	
pl	*nom*	puell-ae	
	acc	puell-as	
	gen	puell-arum	
	dat	puell-is	
	abl	puell-is	

Most first declension nouns are feminine, but a few are masculine, for example *nauta* (= sailor).

• Most of the other exceptions, not included in GCSE, also refer to male jobs or roles: there is no obvious reason for this.

See page 12 on declension and gender. An adjective or participle referring to a masculine first declension noun must be masculine (*nauta bonus* = a good sailor): see page 27 on agreement of nouns and adjectives.

There is no neuter version of the first declension.

The nominative and ablative singular both end in -*a*, but they differ in pronunciation. In the nominative the *a* is short, as in *bat*; in the ablative it is long, as in *father*.

Note also that the genitive and dative singular and the nominative plural endings are all the same (-*ae*). Ambiguous forms have to be worked out from the context.

SECOND DECLENSION NOUNS

Pattern of endings:

sg	nom	-us*	(-um *if n, with no separate voc*)
	acc	-um	
	gen	-i	
	dat	-o	
	abl	-o	
	(*voc	-e)	

pl	nom	-i	(-a *if n*)
	acc	-os	(-a *if n*)
	gen	-orum	
	dat	-is	
	abl	-is	

		master	war
		m	*n*
sg	nom	domin-us*	bell-um
	acc	domin-um	bell-um
	gen	domin-i	bell-i
	dat	domin-o	bell-o
	abl	domin-o	bell-o
	(*voc	domin-e: see page 4)	
pl	nom	domin-i	bell-a
	acc	domin-os	bell-a
	gen	domin-orum	bell-orum
	dat	domin-is	bell-is
	abl	domin-is	bell-is

Nouns like *dominus* required for GCSE are all masculine.

Note that with nouns like *dominus* the genitive singular is the same as the nominative plural, and that with all second declension nouns the dative is like the ablative, both in the singular and in the plural. With neuter nouns like *bellum* the nominative is like the accusative. Ambiguous forms have to be worked out from the context.

• Note that *locus* (= place) is masculine in the singular, but has a neuter plural *loca*.

Second declension masculine nouns with nominative singular ending in -*r* behave as if -*us* had disappeared:

		man	boy
		m	*m*
sg	*nom*	vir	puer
	acc	vir-um	puer-um
	gen	vir-i	puer-i
		etc	*etc*

As a further slight variant, the following is similar to *puer*, but loses the -*e*- from the stem after the nominative (reflecting the fact that it would be dropped in pronunciation):

		book
		m
sg	*nom*	liber
	acc	libr-um
	gen	libr-i
		etc

Note the following special expressions involving first and second declension nouns:

poenas do   I pay the penalty (*literally* give penalties), I am punished
bellum gero I wage war

Exercise 3   First and second declension nouns

1   nauta villam in insula aedificavit.
2   pueri dona in templum deae portabant.
3   filius liberti cibum rogavit.
4   turba virorum in foro adest.
5   muros tabernae celeriter delevimus.
6   femina epistulam mariti non intellexit.
7   Romani multos annos bellum gerebant.
8   verba ancillae domino tandem persuaserunt.
9   servus scelestus poenas dare debet.
10   vir librum legere volebat.

THIRD DECLENSION NOUNS

This is slightly more difficult as the nominative singular can end in many different ways, but the endings for the other cases (added to the *stem*, as explained below) again follow a definite pattern.

Pattern of endings:			
sg	*nom*	(*wide range of possibilities*)	
	acc	-em	(*same as nom if n*)
	gen	-is	
	dat	-i	
	abl	-e	
pl	*nom*	-es	(-a *if n*)
	acc	-es	(-a *if n*)
	gen	-(i)um	
	dat	-ibus	
	abl	-ibus	

		king	shout	ship	name
		m	*m*	*f*	*n*
sg	*nom*	rex	clamor	nav-is	nomen
	acc	reg-em	clamor-em	nav-em	nomen
	gen	reg-is	clamor-is	nav-is	nomin-is
	dat	reg-i	clamor-i	nav-i	nomin-i
	abl	reg-e	clamor-e	nav-e	nomin-e
pl	*nom*	reg-es	clamor-es	nav-es	nomin-a
	acc	reg-es	clamor-es	nav-es	nomin-a
	gen	reg-um	clamor-um	nav-ium	nomin-um
	dat	reg-ibus	clamor-ibus	nav-ibus	nomin-ibus
	abl	reg-ibus	clamor-ibus	nav-ibus	nomin-ibus

For masculine and feminine words, form and gender are not necessarily connected: many feminine nouns follow a pattern similar to *rex*, and many masculine ones decline like *navis*.

With first and second declension nouns (see pages 13–17), the nominative singular always shows what the stem is (for example *dominus*, stem *domin-*). This works for some third declension nouns (for example *clamor*, where the nominative simply is the stem, or *navis*, where the ending *-is* can easily be removed to show the stem *nav-*), but often the nominative is changed a bit, so that the stem is concealed (for example *rex*, concealing the stem *reg-*).

As well as the nominative therefore you always need to know the stem of a third declension noun, in order to work out the other bits. (This is less of a problem than it may seem: nouns within the third declension fall into subgroups, and when you have seen a few you can often predict the stem. Also, English derivatives often give a clue to the stem: thus *military* from *miles*, stem *milit-*).

Nouns of all declensions are usually quoted in lists and dictionaries with the nominative and genitive singular (see the vocabulary in the back of this book: pages 184–98). This is particularly important for third declension nouns, where the genitive shows the stem. We use the genitive for this purpose because quoting the accusative would be fine for masculine and feminine nouns, but would not work for neuter ones, where the stem is not used until we get to the genitive. So for example:

miles, militis *m*   soldier

The genitive *militis* shows that the stem is *milit-*. Often an abbreviated form is used to save space, not repeating the syllable or syllables that stay the same:

miles, -itis (*for* militis) *m*   guard
flumen, -inis (*for* fluminis) *n*   river

Nominative, stem, and gender give all the information needed to work out any bit of a regular noun.

• Note that the genitive plural in the third declension is sometimes *-um*, sometimes *-ium*. A rule that explains most examples of this distinction says that the genitive plural should be one syllable longer than the nominative singular: if the genitive singular is already one syllable longer (as with *rex* or *clamor*), there is no need to increase it again for the genitive plural (so it is *-um*), but if there is no increase in the singular (as with *navis*), there has to be in the plural (so it is *-ium*). But there are exceptions. Many words whose nominative singular is a single syllable, for example *urbs* (= city) increase twice: *urbs*, *urbis*, *urbium* (though *rex* does not).

All nominative and accusative plurals in the third declension (and as usual also nominative and accusative neuter singulars) are *ambiguous* forms: you cannot tell in isolation which case they are, but context and word order normally enable you to work it out. So for example:

cives nuntios laudant.
The citizens praise the messengers.

Here the second declension *nuntios* is accusative, so *cives* must be nominative.

nuntii cives laudant.
The messengers praise the citizens.

Here the second declension *nuntii* is nominative, so *cives* must be accusative.

• There are also possibilities for confusion with endings of other declensions. The third declension genitive plural ending in *-um* or *-ium* might be mistaken for a second declension accusative singular such as *dominum* or *filium*. The third declension nominative or genitive singular *-is* might be mistaken for the dative or ablative plural of a first or second declension noun (though those endings have a long *i* and so are pronounced differently). As with any neuter plural ending in *-a*, there is the risk of confusion with a first declension noun like *puella* (but if the neuter plural is nominative it will of course have a plural verb). Thorough learning of both vocabulary and declensions is the safest way to avoid such problems, but intelligent deduction from sense and context will also take you a long way.

• Note that the following third declension nouns are usually masculine, but can also be feminine, according to the sex of the people described (by convention a mixed group is regarded as masculine):

civis, -is   citizen
comes, -itis   companion
custos, -odis   guard

Exercise 4   Third declension nouns

1 milites vocem imperatoris audire non poterant.
2 nonne nomen custodis cognovisti?
3 multae naves ab hostibus delebantur.
4 frater senatoris fortissimus erat.
5 eo tempore duo legiones ibi pugnabant.
6 iter difficile per montes ad mare facere debebimus.
7 pater regis a custodibus servatus est.
8 canis militis corpus eius per totam noctem custodiebat.
9 vulnera senis sanguine celata sunt.
10 princeps matrem meam laudavit.

Exercise 5   First, second and third declension nouns (revision)

1 liberti in taberna diu laborabant.
2 senex uxorem saepe laudabat.
3 comites nostrae in horto iacent.
4 naves regis trans omnia maria navigant.
5 domina mea epistulam filio misit.
6 cives periculum belli diu timebant.
7 per silvam ad flumen ambulabam.
8 consiliumne novum habet dux noster?
9 servus ianuam villae mihi ostendit.
10 cur templum deae non intravisti?

FOURTH AND FIFTH DECLENSION NOUNS

These are much less common than the first three declensions. There are only a few of each, but they include some important words. Fourth declension can be thought of as a variant of second, and fifth as a variant of third.

		FOURTH DECLENSION	FIFTH DECLENSION
		hand, *or* group of people	day
		f	*m (or f)*
sg	nom	man-us	di-es
	acc	man-um	di-em
	gen	man-us	di-ei
	dat	man-ui	di-ei
	abl	man-u	di-e
pl	nom	man-us	di-es
	acc	man-us	di-es
	gen	man-uum	di-erum
	dat	man-ibus	di-ebus
	abl	man-ibus	di-ebus

The two different meanings of *manus* are linked by the idea of a group of people as a *handful*.

There are both masculine and feminine nouns in both the fourth and the fifth declension (there is also a neuter version of fourth, but there are no examples in the GCSE vocabulary).

Four different bits of a word like *manus* (nominative and genitive singular, nominative and accusative plural) are spelled in the same way (the *u* in the nominative singular is pronounced short, the others long). The number and case have to be worked out from the context. Note in particular that if the word is accusative, it must also be plural:

hic servus magnas manus habet.
This slave has big hands.

• Note that *domus* (= house) has the ablative singular *domo* (and usually the accusative plural *domos*) as if it were second declension: see page 15, and page 63 for its locative *domi*.

• Note that *dies* is usually masculine, but in the singular can be feminine if it refers to a special day.

• Note that *res* has a range of meanings: *thing, business*, but also *story* (*totam rem narravit* = he told the whole story).

Exercise 6   Fourth and fifth declension nouns

1   nullam spem pacis habemus.
2   frater meus paucis diebus adveniet.
3   nuntius vultu misero totam rem regi narravit.
4   cuius manu scripta est haec epistula?
5   manum militum prope domum manentem conspeximus.

ADJECTIVES

There are two basic types: one which is a mixture of first and second declensions (second in the masculine and neuter, first in the feminine), and another which is third declension (with masculine and feminine the same, and a variant form for the neuter).

		FIRST AND SECOND DECLENSION (2-1-2)		
		good		
		m	*f*	*n*
sg	*nom*	bon-us*	bon-a	bon-um
	acc	bon-um	bon-am	bon-um
	gen	bon-i	bon-ae	bon-i
	dat	bon-o	bon-ae	bon-o
	abl	bon-o	bon-a	bon-o
	(**voc*	bon-e)		
pl	*nom*	bon-i	bon-ae	bon-a
	acc	bon-os	bon-as	bon-a
	gen	bon-orum	bon-arum	bon-orum
	dat	bon-is	bon-is	bon-is
	abl	bon-is	bon-is	bon-is

This is exactly like the three nouns *dominus, puella, bellum* (see pages 13 and 15). Nouns are usually dealt with in declension order (first, second) but for adjectives the convention is to set them out in gender order: masculine, feminine, neuter.

• A similar layout is used for pronouns (pages 40–60) and participles (pages 118–27).

This set of forms is very important: it is used in many different contexts and will be referred to constantly. Understanding it thoroughly means a big reduction in mechanical learning. It is described in this book as *2-1-2*. This is shorthand for *2m-1f-2n*: second declension masculine like *dominus*, first declension feminine like *puella*, second declension neuter like *bellum* (there is no need to quote the genders each time because the order is always *m, f, n*).

• This type of adjective is normally quoted in lists and dictionaries as *bonus -a -um*, giving in abbreviated form the nominative singulars for the three genders.

Note that for the masculine and feminine forms here, gender and declension are in effect equated: each gender uses the endings of the declension where most of the nouns belong to that gender (see page 12 on gender and declension).

There are a few adjectives with masculine nominative singular ending -er (compare the nouns on page 16):

> *miser* (= miserable) keeps the *e* like *puer* does, hence accusative *miserum*; *pulcher* (= beautiful) drops the *e* like *liber* does, hence accusative *pulchrum*.

For the third declension type, it is useful to study two models (others can be worked out):

THIRD DECLENSION			
		brave, strong	
		m/f	*n*
sg	*nom*	fort-is	fort-e
	acc	fort-em	fort-e
	gen	fort-is	fort-is
	dat	fort-i	fort-i
	abl	fort-i	fort-i
pl	*nom*	fort-es	fort-ia
	acc	fort-es	fort-ia
	gen	fort-ium	fort-ium
	dat	fort-ibus	fort-ibus
	abl	fort-ibus	fort-ibus

The masculine/feminine version of this is almost identical to the noun *navis* (see page 18), but note that *fortis*, like most third declension adjectives, has -*i* (instead of the -*e* which the nouns have) in the ablative singular. The form *forte* is used instead for the neuter: see page 35 for the potential confusion with the unconnected adverb *forte* (= by chance). As usual with neuter words, the nominative and accusative (in both singular and plural) are the same as each other, and the nominative and accusative plural end in -*a* (here -*ia*: compare how the genitive plural is -*ium* rather than -*um*, and see page 19).

• This type of adjective is normally quoted as *fortis -e*, giving the two nominative singular endings, *m/f* and *n*.

• Note that *celer* (= swift) is third declension and behaves as if it had started *celeris* (and in fact does so in the feminine, which here unusually differs from the masculine).

THIRD DECLENSION			
		huge	
		m/f	*n*
sg	*nom*	ingens	ingens
	acc	ingent-em	ingens
	gen	ingent-is	ingent-is
	dat	ingent-i	ingent-i
	abl	ingent-i	ingent-i
pl	*nom*	ingent-es	ingent-ia
	acc	ingent-es	ingent-ia
	gen	ingent-ium	ingent-ium
	dat	ingent-ibus	ingent-ibus
	abl	ingent-ibus	ingent-ibus

• This type of adjective (unlike the others, but like a third declension noun) is normally quoted as *ingens -entis*, giving the nominative and genitive singular forms: these are the same for all three genders but the stem *ingent-* (which cannot be worked out from the nominative) needs to be shown.

• Note that, although the nominative singular is the same for all three genders, the neuter differs by repeating this form for the accusative (because all neuter words have nominative and accusative the same).

• Closely resembling *ingens* are *diligens* (= careful) and *sapiens* (= wise), but other adjectives follow a comparable pattern: *audax -acis* (= bold), *felix -icis* (= lucky) with its opposite *infelix -icis* (= unlucky), and *ferox -ocis* (= fierce).

• The present active participle (see page 118) also follows the model of *ingens*.

AGREEMENT OF NOUNS AND ADJECTIVES

Every adjective must *agree* with the noun it refers to in number, gender and case. If a noun is first or second declension *and* the adjective is of 2-1-2 form, the endings will often actually be identical: for example *amicos bonos* = good friends (accusative plural). This will often be true as well if the noun is third declension *and* the adjective also is: for example *militem fortem* = a brave soldier (accusative singular). But exact matching of forms (or 'rhyming') like this is a bonus: it is NOT what *agreeing* means. The adjective must follow the gender of the noun, and it must be in the right number and case. Sometimes that will produce an identical ending, sometimes not.

Adjectives normally come after the noun they refer to. But a few common ones (most of them referring to size or quantity) usually come in front, like English adjectives do:

magnus -a -um	big
parvus -a -um	small
multus -a -um	much, *pl* many
pauci -ae -a	few
omnis -e	all
novus -a -um	new

Note also that any adjective can be used on its own *as* a noun: in such cases a suitable noun has to be *supplied* in English from the grammar and context:

nuntius multa dixit.
The messenger said many *things*.

dea bonos amat.
The goddess loves good *men/people* (or the good, *as a category*).

Here there is no separate words for *things* or *men/people*: they have to be worked out and supplied from the fact that *multa* is neuter, *bonos* is masculine, and both are plural.

• Note that the adjectives *medius -a -um* (= middle) and *summus -a -um* (= highest, top) are often used to mean *middle/top of*, i.e. *summus mons* usually means *the top of the mountain*, rather than *the highest mountain* (of several).

Exercise 7   Agreement of nouns and adjectives

1   nauta Romanus a servo audaci necatus est.
2   senex bonus librum brevem scripsit.
3   rex pessimus multa dira fecit.
4   cives stulti equum infelicem in urbem duxerunt.
5   clamor ingens ab omnibus pueris audiebatur.

COMPARATIVE ADJECTIVES

A *comparative* adjective is used to compare two people or things, to express the fact that one has a particular quality to a greater extent than another. In English a comparative is usually formed by adding -*er* to a short word (*long* becomes *longer*), or putting *more* in front of a longer word (*complicated* becomes *more complicated*).

		longer	
		m/f	*n*
sg	*nom*	longior	longius
	acc	longior-em	longius
	gen	longior-is	longior-is
	dat	longior-i	longior-i
	abl	longior-e	longior-e
pl	*nom*	longior-es	longior-a
	acc	longior-es	longior-a
	gen	longior-um	longior-um
	dat	longior-ibus	longior-ibus
	abl	longior-ibus	longior-ibus

The syllable -*ior* is added to the basic stem, and the comparative form is third declension (see pages 18 and 25–6). This applies regardless of whether the ordinary adjective is 2-1-2 (as *longus* is) or third declension (like for example *fortis*). Note that the ablative here is -*e*, like the nouns (see page 25). Irregular comparatives (see page 33) use these same endings.

• Note the distinctive neuter form (which might be mistaken for a second declension masculine form like *filius*): this is also used for the comparative *adverb* (see page 38).

A comparative adjective is very often followed by *quam* (= than). The two people or things being compared will be in the same case. In a simple comparison this is often nominative:

> dominus stultior est quam servus.
> The master is more stupid than the slave (is).

But they can be in any case, according to their job in the sentence:

> senex librum multo longiorem mihi quam fratri dedit.
> The old man gave a much longer book to me than (he gave) to
> my brother.

• The adverb *multo* (= [by] much) is often used with a comparative to stress the amount of difference.

A simple comparison can alternatively be expressed by missing out *quam* and putting the second noun in the ablative (*ablative of comparison*):

> dominus stultior est servo.
> *lit*   The master is more stupid, by (the side of *or* the standard of) the slave.
> *i.e.*   The master is more stupid than the slave.

SUPERLATIVE ADJECTIVES

A *superlative* adjective tells us that a person or thing has a quality to a very great extent, or to the greatest extent of any in a group. In English the first meaning is expressed by using *very*, the second usually by adding *-est* to a short word (*long* becomes *longest*), or putting *most* in front of a long word (*complicated* becomes *most complicated*).

		longest, very long		
		m	*f*	*n*
sg	*nom*	longissim-us	longissim-a	longissim-um
	acc	longissim-um	longissim-am	longissim-um
		etc	*etc*	*etc*

The syllables *-issim-* are added to the basic stem, and the superlative is regular 2-1-2 in form (see page 24). This applies regardless of whether the ordinary adjective is 2-1-2 (as *longus* is) or third declension (like for example *fortis*). Irregular superlatives (see page 33) use these same endings.

The context usually enables you to tell whether *very* or *-est/most* is the appropriate translation.

> quod epistulam tuam acceperat, puella laetissima erat.
> Because she had received your letter, the girl was very happy.

> hic servus stultissimus omnium est.
> This slave is the most stupid of all (the slaves).

The use of a genitive plural after a superlative, as in the second example, is a reliable indication that *the most . . .* is needed in English.

Exercise 8   Comparative and superlative adjectives (regular)

1 librum difficiliorem numquam legi.
2 miles ferocissimus puerum terruit.
3 hic servus fidelior est quam ceteri.
4 mare illo die saevissimum erat.
5 libertus nunc laetior est quam dominus a quo liberatus est.
6 haec via brevissima est.
7 ille senex sapientior est quam filius.
8 milites Romani audacissimi sunt.
9 hic puer fortior est fratre.
10 montem altissimum in insula conspeximus.

IRREGULAR COMPARATIVE AND SUPERLATIVE ADJECTIVES

An adjective is often shown with its comparative and superlative forms:

ordinary form		*comparative*	*superlative*
longus	*long*	longior	longissimus

This is particularly useful if they are irregular. A number of adjectives have slightly irregular superlatives that are still very easy to recognise.

• 2-1-2 adjectives with masculine nominative singular ending *-er* (and the third declension *celer*) have the superlative ending *-errimus*:

miser	*miserable*	miserior	miserrimus
pulcher	*beautiful*	pulchrior	pulcherrimus
celer	*swift*	celerior	celerrimus

• A few third declension adjectives with masculine/feminine nominative singular ending *-ilis* have the superlative ending *-illimus*:

facilis	*easy*	facilior	facillimus
difficilis	*difficult*	difficilior	difficillimus

More care needs to be taken with the very irregular forms. Note that these are often irregular in English too. In language generally, the most common words are typically the most irregular, because they have got bashed around with use. They quickly become familiar because they are met so often.

bonus	*good*	melior	*better*	optimus	*best*
malus	*bad*	peior	*worse*	pessimus	*worst*
magnus	*big*	maior	*bigger*	maximus	*biggest*
parvus	*small*	minor	*smaller*	minimus	*smallest*
multus	*much*	plus	*more (of)*	plurimus	*most (of)*
multi	*many*	plures	*more*	plurimi	*most*

• Note that *plus* in the singular behaves like a neuter noun meaning *a greater amount*, for example *plus cibi* (= more food): see page 7.

Exercise 9 Comparative and superlative adjectives (irregular)

1 plurimi nautae in foro aderant.
2 senator quidam domum maximam aedificavit.
3 puellam pulcherrimam heri vidi.
4 pater plus pecuniae mihi quam fratri meo dedit.
5 consilium tuum melius meo est.
6 plures milites in silva quam in castris manebant.
7 lux iter facillimum fecit.
8 peiorem servum numquam vidi.
9 rex terram minimam habebat.
10 librum optimum nunc habeo.

ADVERBS

Adverbs usually describe verbs, just as adjectives describe nouns (adverbs can also describe adjectives, or other adverbs).

(1) Many adverbs have a corresponding adjective, from which they are formed.

We had a slow journey.	*adjective*
We travelled slowly.	*adverb*

As this example illustrates, adverbs formed from adjectives in English often end *-ly* (though we cannot for example say *difficultly*, but have to use a more roundabout expression: *with difficulty* or *in a difficult way*).

For 2-1-2 adjectives (see page 24) the adverb is formed by removing *-us* from the masculine nominative singular and <u>adding *-e* to the stem</u>. So for example:

laetus	happy	*adjective*
laete	happily	*adverb*

- Note that the adverb from *bonus* (= good) is *bene* (= well).

For third declension adjectives (see pages 25–6) the adverb is formed by <u>adding *-iter* to the stem</u>. So for example:

brevis	brief	*adjective*
breviter	briefly	*adverb*

- Sometimes the *i* in the ending is dropped and just *-ter* is added to the stem: *audax* (= bold), stem *audac-*, adverb *audacter*. If the stem already ends in *t* just *-er* is added: *sapiens* (= wise), stem *sapient-*, adverb *sapienter*.

- Although *facilis* (= easy) and *difficilis* (= difficult) are third declension, they form their adverbs by adding *-e*: hence *facile*, *difficile*.

- Note that the adverb from *fortis* (= brave *or* strong) is *fortiter*. The adverb *forte* (= by chance) is unconnected: it comes from the same root as *fortune* in English. Confusion of these two words is a very common mistake in GCSE: see page 164. (The form *forte* could be the neuter nominative or accusative of *fortis*, but this is much less likely to be met than the adverb *by chance*.)

Exercise 10   Adverbs (from adjectives)

1 puella donum laete accepit.
2 senex breviter respondit.
3 dominus servis benigne locutus est.
4 nonne tu pecuniam fideliter custodire potes?
5 omnes fortiter pugnaverunt.
6 quis illa verba stulte scripsit?
7 dominus e villa irate discessit.
8 puer pecuniam senis audacter et crudeliter rapuit.
9 rex civibus omnia haec vere promisit.
10 hostes urbem nostram saeve oppugnaverunt.

(2) There are many other adverbs, not formed from adjectives, that indicate (for example) *when*, *why* or *how* something happens:

antea	before, previously	nunc	now
cras	tomorrow	olim	once, some time ago
deinde	then, next		
diu	for a long time	paene	almost
forte	by chance	postea	afterwards
frustra	in vain	postridie	on the next day
heri	yesterday	saepe	often
hic	here	satis	enough
hodie	today	semper	always
iam	now, already	sic	thus, in this way
ibi	there	statim	at once, immediately
ita	so, in this way		
iterum	again	subito	suddenly
mox	soon	tandem	at last
numquam	never	tum	then

• Other adverbs are explained with the construction of which they form part: question words (for example *cur* = why?) with direct questions (page 105), signpost words (for example *tam* = so) with result clauses (page 146).

Exercise 11   Adverbs (not formed from adjectives)

1   nuntius media nocte forte advenit.
2   nihil postea audivimus.
3   omnia iam parata sunt.
4   pecunia diu quaerebatur.
5   de his rebus satis scio.
6   haec navis iam plena est.
7   illum librum saepe lego.
8   frater meus mox adveniet.
9   Romam frustra festinavimus.
10   hostes urbem iterum oppugnaverunt.

COMPARATIVE AND SUPERLATIVE ADVERBS

The comparative form of an adverb formed from an adjective is the *neuter singular* of the comparative adjective (nominative/accusative form): the distinctive but misleading ending *-ius* (see page 29). Hence for example:

comparative   laetius   more happily

Because a superlative adjective is 2-1-2 in declension (see pages 24 and 31), the adverb form of it is predictably formed in the same way as the adverb of a normal 2-1-2 adjective: remove *-us* from the masculine nominative singular and add *-e* (see page 35). So for example:

superlative   laetissime   very happily, most happily

These rules apply to irregular as well as regular comparatives and superlatives.

A comparative adverb is often followed by *quam* (= than), just as a comparative adjective is (see page 29):·

    senator civibus facilius persuasit quam ego.
    The senator persuaded the citizens more easily than I (did).

Note a different meaning of *quam* when it is attached to a superlative adverb:

quam celerrime   as quickly as possible

• Some adverbs not formed from adjectives (see page 36) have a comparative and superlative following the same pattern. Note in particular:

	diu	for a long time	saepe	often
comparative	diutius	for a longer time	saepius	more often
superlative	diutissime	for a very long time	saepissime	very/most often

Exercise 12 Comparative and superlative adverbs

1 femina epistulam difficilem optime scripsit.
2 nova ancilla melius loquitur quam omnes aliae.
3 pueri cenam quam celerrime consumpserunt.
4 talia nunc saepius accidunt quam antea.
5 cives nuntium laetissime acceperunt.
6 rex homini scelesto iratissime respondit.
7 nemo fortius pugnavit quam dux noster.
8 iuvenes Romani maxime gaudebant.
9 ego celeriter cucurri, sed servus celerius effugit.
10 muri a militibus fortissime custodiebantur.

PRONOUNS

A pronoun is a word such as *I*, *she*, *they* that stands in place of a noun and avoids the need to repeat it.

Some of the common pronouns in English are the only words that have case endings like Latin:

I (*nominative*) changes to me (*accusative*)
he him
she her
they them
who whom (*though this is falling out of use*)

Nominative pronouns are omitted in Latin if the subject of a sentence can be worked out from the verb ending.

Words such as *this* and *that* are classed as pronouns, though when used with a noun they become adjectives. *Possessives*, words indicating the person something belongs to (*my*, *your*), are also included here, though they are normally used as adjectives.

Latin has a lot of pronouns. Confusion over some of the less common ones is a very common mistake in GCSE. On the other hand, pronouns are formed according to fixed patterns (explained below), cutting down the amount of learning needed.

Summary list of pronouns for basic recognition:

ego (*acc* me)	I (me)
nos	we
tu	you (*sg*)
vos	you (*pl*)
is, ea, id	he, she, it
se	him/her/itself
hic	this
ille	that
ipse	self
idem	the same
qui	who
quis	who?
quidam	a certain
alter	one/the other of two
ceteri	the rest
nemo	no-one

PERSONAL PRONOUNS

FIRST PERSON

		I, me, *pl* we, us
sg	*nom*	ego
	acc	me
	gen	mei
	dat	mihi
	abl	me
pl	*nom*	nos
	acc	nos
	gen	nostrum
	dat	nobis
	abl	nobis

SECOND PERSON

		you (*sg and pl*)
sg	*nom*	tu
	acc	te
	gen	tui
	dat	tibi
	abl	te
pl	*nom*	vos
	acc	vos
	gen	vestrum
	dat	vobis
	abl	vobis

First and second person pronouns in the nominative are normally used only for emphasis or to draw a contrast, as the subject can be worked out from the verb ending:

nos semper laboramus.
We are always working (*implying* but others are not).

ego dicam, et tu audies.
I shall speak, and you will listen.

In the other cases they can be used in a reflexive sense (referring back to a first or second person subject):

gladio me defendo.
I defend myself with a sword.

The accusative is often used in this reflexive way as the subject of an infinitive in indirect statement (see pages 132–7):

promisi me rediturum esse.
I promised that I would return.

When these pronouns in the ablative are used with the preposition *cum* (= with), it is stuck on the end (*mecum, tecum, nobiscum, vobiscum*): see below, and page 62.

• For the associated possessive adjectives *meus, noster, tuus, vester* (= my, our, your) see page 45.

THIRD PERSON REFLEXIVE

	himself, herself, itself, *pl* themselves
sg and pl	
	(*no nom*)
acc	se
gen	sui
dat	sibi
abl	se

Note that *se* cannot be translated in isolation, but only in its context in a sentence. It always refers back to the subject, and gets its gender and number from there.

puella sibi cenam paravit.
The girl prepared dinner for herself.

Like the first and second person pronouns, *se* when used in the ablative with the preposition *cum* (= with) has it stuck on the end:

imperator matrem secum duxit.
The emperor took his mother with him.

- For the associated possessive adjective *suus* (= his/her/its/their own) see page 46.

- The reflexive *se* (always third person, and never nominative) must be distinguished carefully from *ipse* (= self) which does not have these restrictions: see page 51.

- For the use of *se* as the subject of an infinitive in indirect statement see page 136.

- With some verbs the reflexive is used in Latin but not translated (English just uses the verb in an intransitive sense):

puer in templo se celavit.
The boy hid in the temple.

This applies also to first and second person reflexives.

THIRD PERSON

he, she, it, *pl* they, them (*can also mean* that, those)

		m	f	n
sg	nom	is	ea	id
	acc	eum	eam	id
	gen	eius	eius	eius
	dat	ei	ei	ei
	abl	eo	ea	eo
pl	nom	ei	eae	ea
	acc	eos	eas	ea
	gen	eorum	earum	eorum
	dat	eis	eis	eis
	abl	eis	eis	eis

Note the distinctive genitive and dative singular endings (*-ius* and *-i*), across all three genders. These are also used for many other pronouns, and are similarly underlined in other tables of pronouns in this book (and the number *one*: see page 107).

Note that the plural is regular 2-1-2 in declension (see page 24).

• This pronoun can also be used with a noun to mean *that*, like *ille* (see page 48).

• The adverbs *antea* (= before, previously) and *postea* (= afterwards) are in origin the pronouns *ante* and *post* plus the neuter plural *ea* (see pages 61 and 109–10).

• For the genitive of this pronoun used as a possessive (*his, hers, its, their*) see pages 46–7.

Exercise 13   Personal pronouns

 1   tu miles eris, ego nauta.
 2   puellae in silva se celaverunt.
 3   ego celerius currere possum quam vos omnes.
 4   num pater me hic videbit?
 5   liberi cenam sibi parabant.
 6   tune librum scripsisti?
 7   rex nobis praemium dedit.
 8   paucos vestrum antea vidi.
 9   nihil tibi offerre possumus, sceleste.
10   dea hominibus se olim ostendit.

POSSESSIVES

A possessive indicates who something belongs to (e.g. *my*, *your*). Most of these are straightforward and decline as 2-1-2 adjectives (see page 24).

FIRST PERSON

my

		m	*f*	*n*
sg	*nom*	meus	mea	meum
	acc	meum	meam	meum
		etc	*etc*	*etc*

our

		m	*f*	*n*
sg	*nom*	noster	nostra	nostrum
	acc	nostrum	nostram	nostrum
		etc	*etc*	*etc*

SECOND PERSON

your (belonging to you *sg*)

		m	*f*	*n*
sg	*nom*	tuus	tua	tuum
	acc	tuum	tuam	tuum
		etc	*etc*	*etc*

your (belonging to you *pl*)

		m	*f*	*n*
sg	*nom*	vester	vestra	vestrum
	acc	vestrum	vestram	vestrum
		etc	*etc*	*etc*

In the third person it is a bit more complicated. There are two different ways of expressing *his/her/its/their*, according to whether or not the possessive refers back to the subject of the sentence. If it does, the adjective *suus* is used:

THIRD PERSON REFLEXIVE			
	his/her/its/their (own) (*belonging to whoever is the subject of the sentence*)		
	m	*f*	*n*
sg nom	suus	sua	suum
acc	suum	suam	suum
	etc	*etc*	*etc*
	(regular 2-1-2: see page 24)		

Note that *suus* cannot be translated out of context. Its meaning depends on who is the subject of the sentence. Its number and gender are those of the thing possessed, not the possessor. Thus it is NOT the case, as you might think, that the masculine means *his*, the feminine *her*, and the plural *their*: any part of *suus* can mean any of these, depending on the number and gender of the subject.

• Note the use of *suos* (masculine plural, without a noun), usually meaning *his men* (i.e. soldiers):

> imperator suos in periculum duxit.
> The general led his men into danger.

Alternatively it may refer to a mixed group, and take its meaning from the subject and context (*literally* his/her/their own people):

> puella capta promisit suos pecuniam missuros esse.
> The girl who had been captured promised that her family would send money.

When the reference of *his/her/its/their* is to someone other than the subject, there is no adjective and so the genitive of the pronoun *is, ea, id* (see page 43) is used instead: literally *of him, of her, of it*. This time the number and gender ARE those of the possessor, though in the singular all three genders are the same anyway (*eius*).

• Note carefully that the ending of the possessive *eius* is the distinctive *-ius* genitive of a pronoun (see page 43), NOT the masculine nominative singular of a 2-1-2 adjective, as it is with *suus*.

THIRD PERSON NON-REFLEXIVE

	his/her/its (*belonging to someone who is not the subject of the sentence*)		
	m	*f*	*n*
sg	eius	eius	eius
	their (*belonging to people who are not the subject of the sentence*)		
pl	eorum	earum	eorum

• For the third person non-reflexive possessive, the genitive of a pronoun is used because no adjective is available. Any other possessive could be expressed in this way, but an adjective is used where there is one: *domus mei* (= the house of me) would be intelligible for *my house*, but in practice *domus mea* is used instead.

Exercise 14   Possessives

1   cibus noster semper pessimus est.
2   frater meus libros suos numquam legit.
3   vocem tuam iterum audire nolo.
4   milites duci suo semper credebant.
5   mare nostrum plurimos portus habet.
6   ego hunc senem et uxorem eius heri vidi.
7   frater meus tuum non timet.
8   haec femina et maritum suum et pecuniam eius amat.
9   nonne urbem vestram laudatis, cives?
10   imperator non suum equum sed meum habet.

THIS AND *THAT*

		this, *pl* these		
		m	*f*	*n*
sg	*nom*	hic	haec	hoc
	acc	hunc	hanc	hoc
	gen	huius	huius	huius
	dat	huic	huic	huic
	abl	hoc	hac	hoc
pl	*nom*	hi	hae	haec
	acc	hos	has	haec
	gen	horum	harum	horum
	dat	his	his	his
	abl	his	his	his

Again note the distinctive genitive and dative singular endings, the dative here adding -*c* to the -*i* that most pronouns have.

The plural is regular 2-1-2 in declension (see page 24) apart from the neuter nominative and accusative (and even this resembles regular 2-1-2 by being the same as the feminine nominative singular).

		that, *pl* those		
		m	*f*	*n*
sg	*nom*	ille	illa	illud
	acc	illum	illam	illud
	gen	illius	illius	illius
	dat	illi	illi	illi
	abl	illo	illa	illo
pl	*nom*	illi	illae	illa
	acc	illos	illas	illa
	gen	illorum	illarum	illorum
	dat	illis	illis	illis
	abl	illis	illis	illis

Again note the distinctive genitive and dative singular endings across all three genders.

The plural is regular 2-1-2 in declension (see page 24).

Note that *this* implies *here, near me*, whereas *that* implies *over there, further away*.

• Note that the third person pronoun *is, ea, id* can also be used as an adjective meaning *that* (i.e. the same as *ille, illa, illud*).

> legistine omnes eos libros?
> Have you read all those books?

The words *this* and *that* illustrate well how pronouns are often used as adjectives. If part of *hic* or *ille* is used with a noun, it usually comes in front of it:

> hic vir nihil nobis dicere potest.   (hic *as adjective*)
> This man can tell us nothing.

But the same meaning could be expressed by *hic* alone:

> hic nobis nihil dicere potest.   (hic *as pronoun*)

A word such as *man, woman, thing, people* is supplied in English according to the gender and number of the pronoun.

> iubeo te omnia illa eicere.
> I order you to throw out all those things.

Often *ille* is used for *he* as the subject of a sentence, referring to someone who was mentioned in the previous sentence but was not its subject:

> dominus servum diu petivit. ille tandem rediit.
> The master looked for the slave for a long time. He (i.e. the slave)
> finally returned.

• For the use of the *connecting relative* in a similar way, as the subject of a new sentence, see pages 116–17.

Exercise 15 *This* and *that*

 1 num omnes has epistulas scripsistis?
 2 dominus huius servi non adest.
 3 clamores illorum civium eam servaverunt.
 4 ille miles semper fortiter pugnat.
 5 hanc solam amo.
 6 ianua illius villae alta est.
 7 hic equus celerior est illo.
 8 ea verba iterum audire nolo.
 9 illa nocte nihil grave accidit.
10 nuntius regis haec mihi dixit.

SELF AND *SAME*

		m	f	n
		self, *pl* selves		
sg	*nom*	ipse	ipsa	ipsum
	acc	ipsum	ipsam	ipsum
	gen	ipsius	ipsius	ipsius
	dat	ipsi	ipsi	ipsi
	abl	ipso	ipsa	ipso
pl	*nom*	ipsi	ipsae	ipsa
	acc	ipsos	ipsas	ipsa
		etc	*etc*	*etc*

(regular 2-1-2 plural: see page 24)

Again note the distinctive genitive and dative singular endings.

Note carefully the distinction between *ipse* and *se* (which is always third person, always reflexive, and never nominative: see page 42). The word *ipse* commonly implies *in person* (not through someone else). Nominative parts of it can be used regardless of person:

nos ipsi nihil audivimus.
We ourselves heard nothing.

Though classed as a pronoun, *ipse* is very often used with a noun or another pronoun:

regem ipsum vidi.
I saw the king himself.

illi ipsi omnia audiverunt.
Those men themselves heard everything.

It can be added to a reflexive (see pages 41–3) for extra emphasis:

hic miles se ipsum semper laudat.
This soldier always praises himself.

		m	*f*	*n*
		the same		
sg	*nom*	idem	eadem	idem
	acc	eundem	eandem	idem
	gen	eiusdem	eiusdem	eiusdem
	dat	eidem	eidem	eidem
	abl	eodem	eadem	eodem
pl	*nom*	eidem	eaedem	eadem
	acc	eosdem	easdem	eadem
	gen	eorundem	earundem	eorundem
	dat	eisdem	eisdem	eisdem
	abl	eisdem	eisdem	eisdem

This is the pronoun *is, ea, id* (see page 43) with *-dem* stuck on the end, and minor adjustments of spelling.* Again note the distinctive genitive and dative singular endings (this time with *-dem* added).

* The *-s* of the masculine nominative singular has disappeared, so *idem* not *isdem*. The neuter ending in *-d* already does not double it (so neuter nominative and accusative singular, like masculine nominative, are *idem*). Any part of the original pronoun ending *-m* changes it to *-n* before *-dem* is added, to ease pronunciation (so masculine accusative singular *eundem*, not *eumdem*).

Like other pronouns, parts of *idem* can be used alone (supplying a suitable noun in English from gender, number and context), or as an adjective with a noun:

hic senex eadem semper dicit.
This old man always says the same things.

num eundem librum iterum legere vis?
Surely you do not want to read the same book again?

Exercise 16   *Self* and *same*

1 num regis ipsius equum habes?
2 hic puer idem semper rogat.
3 consumpsistisne omnes eundem cibum?
4 multa vera de imperatore ipso dicebantur.
5 haec est villa quam ego ipse aedificavi.
6 nonne templum ipse vidisti?
7 omnes naves eodem modo factae sunt.
8 cives nuntium ipsum de bello rogaverunt.
9 omnes eodem die advenerunt.
10 donum reginae ipsi mittere volo.

RELATIVE PRONOUN (*WHO, WHICH*) AND CLAUSE

		who, which		
		m	*f*	*n*
sg	*nom*	qui	quae	quod
	acc	quem	quam	quod
	gen	<u>cuius</u>	<u>cuius</u>	<u>cuius</u>
	dat	<u>cui</u>	<u>cui</u>	<u>cui</u>
	abl	quo	qua	quo
pl	*nom*	qui	quae	quae
	acc	quos	quas	quae
	gen	quorum	quarum	quorum
	dat	quibus	quibus	quibus
	abl	quibus	quibus	quibus

Note that the plural here is 2-1-2 (see page 24) apart from (a) the neuter nominative and accusative (which however resembles 2-1-2 by being the same as the feminine nominative singular) and (b) the dative and ablative for all three genders, which are *quibus*, not *quis*.

The relative pronoun gets its name from the fact that it *relates* or links two facts about a person or thing:

> servus, quem heri vidi, iterum adest.
> The slave, whom I saw yesterday, is here again.

The relative pronoun refers or *relates back* to a noun that usually comes just before it (and so is called the *antecedent* = preceding). The relative pronoun <u>agrees with the antecedent in *number* and *gender* but NOT necessarily in *case*.</u> Its case is determined by the job it is doing in its own clause. A relative clause is in effect one sentence stuck inside another. In the example above, the main sentence is:

> servus iterum adest.
> The slave is here again.

The sentence which has been made into the relative clause would on its own be:

> servum heri vidi.
> I saw the slave yesterday.

If we kept it separate but used a pronoun, it would be:

> eum heri vidi.
> I saw him yesterday.

Clearly *him* has to be accusative as it is the object of *vidi*. This is still true when we put this sentence inside the other one as a relative clause.

Note that in English the singular *who* becomes *whom* in the accusative, and *whose* in the genitive. The word *whom* however is dropping out of use, and *who* is commonly used for the accusative too.

• Alternatively *that* is often used instead (*the slave that I saw*), or the relative pronoun is missed out altogether (*the slave I saw*): these versions are preferred when the relative clause is being used to distinguish this slave from others.

Any combination of cases for antecedent and relative pronoun is possible:

> quaerimus navem quae antea in portu erat.
> We are looking for the ship that was previously in the harbour.

Here the antecedent *navem* is accusative because it is the object of *quaerimus*, and the relative pronoun *quae* is nominative because it is the subject of *erat*.

The relative clause may have both subject and object of its own, with the relative pronoun in another case:

> senex cui puella epistulam misit laetissimus erat.
> The old man to whom the girl sent the letter was very happy.

Here the antecedent *senex* is nominative because it is the subject of *erat*, and the relative pronoun *cui* is dative because if we extracted the clause as a separate sentence, it would be:

> puella seni epistulam misit.
> The girl sent the letter to the old man.

Note that the relative pronoun is often used after parts of the third person pronoun *is, ea, id* (see page 43):

ei qui fugerant mox capti sunt.
Those who had run away were soon captured.

• For the use of *qui, quae, quod* as a connecting relative to link sentences together see page 116.

Exercise 17   Relative pronoun and clause

1   donum quod heri accepi optimum est.
2   videsne pecuniam quae hic iacet?
3   ancilla quam omnes amant pulcherrima est.
4   senex cui epistulam misisti non adest.
5   turba cuius clamores audire possumus irata esse videtur.
6   da mihi equum qui celerior est, imperator!
7   captivi quorum custos eram omnes effugerunt.
8   vulnera quae pro patria passi sumus gravissima erant.
9   hic est liber sine quo nihil facere possum.
10   duces quibus antea credideram fratrem meum non defenderunt.

LESS COMMON PRONOUNS

			who? what?	
		m	*f*	*n*
sg	*nom*	quis	quis	quid
	acc	quem	quem	quid
		(other parts the same as the relative pronoun *qui, quae, quod*: see page 54)		

This is used in direct questions (see page 105), where it comes first word in the sentence, and also in indirect questions (see page 154).

			a, a certain, *pl* some	
		m	*f*	*n*
sg	*nom*	quidam	quaedam	quoddam
	acc	quendam	quandam	quoddam
	gen	cuiusdam	cuiusdam	cuiusdam
	dat	cuidam	cuidam	cuidam
	abl	quodam	quadam	quodam
pl	*nom*	quidam	quaedam	quaedam
	acc	quosdam	quasdam	quaedam
	gen	quorundam	quarundam	quorundam
	dat	quibusdam	quibusdam	quibusdam
	abl	quibusdam	quibusdam	quibusdam

This is the relative pronoun *qui, quae, quod* with *-dam* stuck on the end, and minor adjustments. Again note the distinctive genitive and dative singular endings (this time with *-dam* added).

• Compare how *idem* (see page 52) is the pronoun *is, ea, id* with *-dem* stuck on the end. In forming parts of *quidam* too, any part of the original pronoun ending *-m* changes it to *-n* before *-dam* is added, to ease pronunciation (so masculine accusative singular *quendam*, not *quemdam*). Here the neuter ending *-d* is kept, producing *quoddam*.

Any part of *quidam* can be used alone or with a noun (which it usually follows):

quosdam in summo monte conspexi.
I caught sight of some people on the top of the mountain.

librum quendam quaero.
I am looking for a certain book.

feminae quaedam in via stabant.
Some women were standing in the street.

Exercise 18   Less common pronouns (i)

1   quis pecuniam in silva celavit?
2   verba quaedam audire non poteram.
3   quem in foro heri vidisti?
4   est femina quaedam quam omnes amamus.
5   cui praemium dedisti, domine?
6   nonne novum consilium quoddam habes?
7   cuius est hic gladius?
8   cenam servi cuiusdam auxilio celeriter parare poteramus.
9   quid ibi accidit?
10   nomina quorundam nemo scit.

		one . . . the other (*of two*), another, a/the second		
		m	*f*	*n*
sg	*nom*	alter	altera	alterum
	acc	alterum	alteram	alterum
	gen	alterius	alterius	alterius
	dat	alteri	alteri	alteri
	abl	altero	altera	altero
pl	*nom*	alteri	alterae	altera
	acc	alteros	alteras	altera
		etc	*etc*	*etc*
		(regular 2-1-2 plural: see page 24)		

Again note the distinctive genitive and dative singular forms. This gives us the English word *alternate*. It is often used in a pair, requiring a different translation each time (*one . . . the other*):

> alter liber difficilis est, alter facilis.
> One book is difficult, the other easy.

• Note that *alter* must not be confused with *altus* (= high *or* deep).

The use of *alter . . . alter* implies that just two are involved. If there are more than two, *alius . . . alius* is used. In the singular this is translated *one . . . another*, but it is more often found in the plural as *some . . . others*:

> alii servorum laborabant, alii in taberna sedebant.
> Some of the slaves were working, others were sitting in the pub.

• If forms of *alius* different from each other in gender and/or case are paired, a double statement is made (abbreviated in Latin, as it can be in English):

	alii alia dicunt.
short for	alii^1 alia^1, alii^2 alia^2 dicunt.
	(*where 1 = some people/things, 2 = other people/things*)

literally	Some people say some things, others say other things.
i.e.	Different people say different things.

the rest, the others (*pl only*)			
		m	*f*	*n*
pl	*nom*	ceteri	ceterae	cetera
	acc	ceteros	ceteras	cetera
		etc	*etc*	*etc*
(regular 2-1-2 plural: see page 24)			

• The English *etc* is an abbreviated form of the neuter plural *et cetera* (= and the other things).

		no-one	nothing
		m/f	*n*
sg	*nom*	nemo	nihil (*indeclinable*)
	acc	neminem	
	gen	nullius	
	dat	nemini	
	abl	nullo	

This is formed like a third declension noun (stem *nemin-*), but its genitive and ablative are borrowed from the adjective *nullus* (= no . . ., not any).

Note that the distinctive singular endings used by most pronouns (genitive *-ius*, dative *-i* across all three genders) are also used for the following adjectives that are otherwise regular 2-1-2 in declension:

	alius	other, another, else
	nullus	no . . ., not any
	solus	alone, only
	totus	whole
also	unus	one (see page 107)

Exercise 19   Less common pronouns (ii)

1 nemo nomen senis cognovit.
2 ceteris necatis, unus miles domum advenit.
3 neminem in foro conspexi.
4 alii manserunt, alii fugerunt.
5 hic vir rex totius insulae factus est.
6 nonne pecunia in alio loco celata est?
7 pauci militum effugerunt, ceteri capti sunt.
8 alter frater in urbe regit, alter egressus est.
9 libris nostris ablatis, alios emere debemus.
10 tantum praemium nemini dabo.

PREPOSITIONS

Prepositions are words such as *in, across, to, from*. As their name (literally *placed in front*) indicates, they come in front of a noun (or pronoun) to express movement or position in relation to it. Prepositions in Latin are followed by either the accusative or the ablative. They serve to focus more closely a meaning the case has already (see pages 5–6 on the accusative, and page 10 on the ablative).

Prepositions with the accusative mostly indicate *motion towards* or *through*, whilst those with the ablative mostly indicate either *a position of rest* in a place or *going away from* it.

(1) Prepositions with the accusative:

ad	to, towards, at
ante	before, in front of
apud	among, with, at the house of
circum	around
contra	against
in	into, onto
inter	among, between
per	through, along
post	after, behind
prope	near
propter	on account of, because of
sub	under, beneath
trans	across

Note that with the name of a town or city (or an island small enough to count as one town) the preposition is omitted, but its name is still accusative if the meaning is motion towards (i.e. it is in the case it would have been in if the preposition *had* been there):

Romam festinavimus.
We hurried to Rome.

• The accusative of *domus* (= house, home) is similarly used without a preposition:

domum ire volo.
I want to go home.

This must be distinguished from the locative *domi* (= at home): see page 63.

Because a preposition comes just before the noun it refers to, it can displace an adjective that would otherwise be there, so that the order is *adjective, preposition, noun*:

multas per vias ambulavimus.
We walked along many streets.

Exercise 20   Prepositions with the accusative

1   omnes cives ad forum festinaverunt.
2   custodes circum muros urbis ambulabant.
3   imperator milites in periculum duxit.
4   post cenam dormire volo.
5   Romam mox adveniemus.
6   multas per terras iter feci.
7   pueri prope flumen currebant.
8   frater apud me multos dies manebat.
9   filius regis inter captivos inventus est.
10 hostes trans mare tandem fugerunt.

---

(2) Prepositions with the ablative:

a/ab*	from, away from, by
cum	with
de	from, down from; about
e/ex*	from, out of
in	in, on
pro	in front of, for, in return for
sine	without
sub	under, beneath

*The forms *ab* and *ex* are used if the next word starts with a vowel or an *h*. The shorter forms *a* and *e* are used if the next word starts with a consonant.

Note that *a/ab* is also used for the agent with a passive verb: see page 95.

Note that *in* and *sub* are used both with the accusative and with the ablative. In both cases the accusative version implies *motion*, and the ablative implies *position*.

cives in forum ambulabant.
The citizens walked *into* the forum.

cives in foro multas horas stabant.
The citizens were standing *in* the forum for many hours.

We noted that with the name of a town or city (or an island small enough to count as one town) the preposition is omitted (see page 61). The ablative alone here indicates *motion away from*:

Roma discessimus.
We departed from Rome.

The idea of *rest in* such a place is given by a special form of its name called the *locative* (literally *placing*) case, which with a normal singular word is the same as the genitive:

Romae diu habitabamus.
We lived in Rome for a long time.

• Note also the following irregular locative form:

domi   at home

from *domus*, though not like its genitive but formed as if second declension: see pages 15 and 22–3)

Exercise 21   Prepositions with the ablative

1   audivistine de morte imperatoris?
2   nihil sine pecunia facere possum.
3   quid sub nave inveniemus?
4   clamores ex omni loco audiebantur.
5   cur in castris manetis?
6   hi pro rege fortiter pugnaverunt.
7   templum multo cum labore tandem confectum est.
8   milites Roma profecti sunt.
9   ille nuntius de monte cucurrit.
10   servus quem sequebamur domi a domino inventus est.

PREFIXES AND COMPOUND VERBS

A compound verb has a *prefix* to focus its meaning. Many of the prepositions (pages 61–3) are also used as prefixes to form compound verbs. Note in particular:

a-/ab-	away, from
ad-	to
de-	down, down from
e-/ex-	out, out of
in-	into, in
re-	back, again
trans-	across

• Attaching the prefix sometimes involves a small modification of spelling, usually to make pronunciation easier:

ab + fero *becomes*	aufero	I take away, carry off, steal
re + eo	redeo	I go back, come back, return
re + do	reddo	I give back

• The last two are classic examples of *words easily confused* (see pages 164–5), though note that *return* works as a translation of *reddo* too in some circumstances (e.g. *I returned his book*).

Prefix and preposition often simply reinforce each other, and only one is translated:

	in templum dei ingressi sumus.
literally	We went in into the temple of the god.
i.e.	We went into the temple of the god.

But it is also possible to give two different pieces of information, one in the prefix and one in the preposition:

cives in viam exierunt.
The citizens went out (*implying e.g.* from their houses) into the street.

Most compounds are verbs of motion, but note (and distinguish carefully between) the two compounds of *to be*:

adsum	I am here, I am present	
absum	I am away, I am absent	(*perfect* afui)

• Some compounds are more obvious than others. Note the following compounds of *venio* (= I come): *advenio* (= I arrive), *invenio* (= I find, *literally* I come into/upon), and *pervenio* (= I reach, *literally* I come through *implying* obstacles).

• Note that the vowel in the verb stem sometimes changes when a compound is formed: *conficio* (= I finish, *literally* make together) and *interficio* (= I kill, *literally* make among, i.e. put among the dead) are compounds of *facio*; similarly *accipio* (= I receive, *literally* take to myself) is a compound of *capio*. The compounds of *iacio* (= I throw) shorten the stem to *-icio*: so *eicio* (= I throw out), *inicio* (= I throw in).

• Note that the deponent verb *-gredior* (see page 99) is found *only* in compound forms: so *egredior* (= I go out), *ingredior* (= I enter), *progredior* (= I advance), *regredior* (= I return).

• Note also (i) *pello* (= I drive) with its compounds *expello* (= I drive out) and *repello* (= I drive back); (ii) *rumpo* (= I burst) with its compounds *irrumpo* (= I burst in, *inr-* changing to *irr-* for ease of pronunciation) and *erumpo* (= I burst out)

Exercise 22   Prefixes and compound verbs

1   pueri libros in flumen iniciebant.
2   omnes senatores nunc adsunt.
3   cives in forum egressi sunt.
4   puellae prope templum convenerunt.
5   uxor senis diu aberat.
6   servus murum conficere coactus est.
7   quis cibum nostrum abstulit?
8   iuvenis domum redire tandem constituit.
9   multae naves ad portum advenerunt.
10   cur pecuniam meam reddere nolebas?

CONJUNCTIONS

A *conjunction* (its name coming from the Latin for *joining together*) connects words or groups of words. Most conjunctions come as the first word in a sentence or clause. Others, often alternatives with similar meaning, come as the second word (as if stitching the sentences or clauses together), but are translated first: these are shown with an asterisk.

et	and	et . . . et	both . . . and
-que	and		
ac *or* atque	and		
sed	but		
autem*	however		
tamen*	however		
nam	for	(giving an explanation)	
enim*	for		
itaque	and so, therefore		
igitur*	therefore		
nec *or* neque	and not, nor, neither		
postquam	after		

Note that there are three different words for *and*: et can join any words or groups of words. The other two usually join things which are felt to belong together (e.g. *land and sea* or *food and wine*): -que is attached to the end of the second word but translated before it:

> libertus fortis fidelisque erat.
> The freedman was brave and faithful.

If *et* is repeated, it is translated *both* the first time:

> rex et nautas et milites habet.
> The king has both sailors and soldiers.

Similarly paired are *nec . . . nec*, or *neque . . . neque* (= neither . . . nor):

> rex neque nautas neque milites habet.
> The king has neither sailors nor soldiers.

- The pronouns *alter . . . alter* and *alii . . . alii* are also often paired: see page 59.

- For the distinction between *post, postea* and *postquam* see pages 109–10.

Exercise 23   Conjunctions

 1   et dominus et servus laetissimi erant.
 2   milites nautaeque a rege laudati sunt.
 3   cibus atque vinum ibi venduntur.
 4   haec insula neque urbes neque flumina habet.
 5   uxor militis mortui tristis erat atque tristis manebit.
 6   postquam in flumen cecidi, saepe clamabam sed nemo audivit.
 7   mater mea nunc laeta est. domum enim novam habet.
 8   nihil accidit. alteram igitur epistulam misi.
 9   Romani post bellum gaudebant. mox tamen iterum oppugnati sunt.
10   naves deletae sunt. itaque cives effugere non poterant.

VERBS AND CONJUGATIONS

Endings (see pages xvi–xvii) are particularly important here as they can give several different pieces of information. Take an example:

festinabamus
we were hurrying

This word can be broken up into four bits:

(1) festin-   the verb stem meaning *hurry*
(2) -a-   the characteristic vowel for first conjugation (see page 71)
(3) -ba-   the syllable that identifies the imperfect tense (see page 71)
(4) -mus   the basic person ending meaning *we* (see below)

Latin verbs fall into four main patterns called *conjugations* (= joined together, i.e. families of verbs). These resemble (and are the origin of) *-er*, *-ir* and *-re* verbs in French.

The example verbs used in this book are:

first conjugation	porto	I carry
second	moneo	I warn
third	traho	I drag
fourth	audio	I hear

• Note that some verbs (for example *capio* = I take) are a mixture of third and fourth conjugation (sometimes called '3½'). Their present, future and imperfect tenses are the same as fourth conjugation. But because of their infinitive ending *-ere* (see page 74) they count overall as third. The way they form their perfect tense (see pages 78–9 and 81) is also like third conjugation.

• For further information about conjugations see page 77 on *principal parts*.

Differences in conjugation mainly affect the vowels used within endings. The basic person endings remain the same across all conjugations and across nearly all active tenses (see pages 78–9 for variations in the perfect tense, and page 91 for the conversion from active to passive).

Verbs are usually set out as follows. The numbers 1, 2, 3 refer to persons. First person is *I*, plural *we*. Second person is *you* (both singular and plural: English used to distinguish singular *thou* from plural *ye*). Third person is *he*, *she*, *it*, plural *they*.

		BASIC PERSON ENDINGS
sg	1	-o *or* -m
	2	-s
	3	-t
pl	1	-mus
	2	-tis
	3	-nt

PRESENT TENSE

conjugation		1st	2nd	3rd	4th
		I carry	I warn	I drag	I hear
sg	1	port-o	mon-eo	trah-o	aud-io
	2	port-as	mon-es	trah-is	aud-is
	3	port-at	mon-et	trah-it	aud-it
pl	1	port-amus	mon-emus	trah-imus	aud-imus
	2	port-atis	mon-etis	trah-itis	aud-itis
	3	port-ant	mon-ent	trah-unt	aud-iunt

The present tense is used to describe an action happening now, though Latin also often uses it to give vividness to a story set in the past, the so-called *historic present* (in English we do this only colloquially, for example in telling a joke).

• The conjunction *dum* (= while) introducing a time clause (see page 111) is normally followed by a present tense, though this often needs to be translated as an imperfect.

• For the present passive see page 93, and for the present participle see pages 118–19.

Exercise 24   Present tense

1 frater meus Romam ire cupit.
2 puer flumen timet.
3 milites nostri hostes semper vincunt.
4 cur haec arma portatis?
5 omnes custodes nunc dormiunt.
6 tale vinum numquam emo.
7 ille senator civibus persuadet.
8 amici nostri nunc tandem urbi appropinquant.
9 quid consumis, serve?
10 vulnus habeo sed nihil sentio.

IMPERFECT TENSE

		I was carrying	I was warning	I was dragging	I was hearing
sg	*1*	port-a-bam	mon-e-bam	trah-e-bam	aud-ie-bam
	2	port-a-bas	mon-e-bas	trah-e-bas	aud-ie-bas
	3	port-a-bat	*etc*	*etc*	*etc*
pl	*1*	port-a-bamus			
	2	port-a-batis			
	3	port-a-bant			

Note the characteristic vowel(s) for each conjugation, immediately after the verb stem:

first	*second*	*third*	*fourth*
a	e	e	ie

These are used in other contexts too: in forming the present participle and gerundive (see pages 118–19 and 142), and in a slightly different form for the infinitive (see page 74). The distinctive endings *-bam*, *-bas*, *-bat* make the imperfect tense very easy to recognise.

The word *imperfect* literally means *uncompleted* (not *faulty*, as in modern English). This is because a typical use of the imperfect is to describe an action that was going on when something interrupted it:

> ubi per silvam ambulabamus, corpus mortuum subito invenimus.
> When we were walking through the wood, we suddenly found a dead body.

The imperfect is also used for any action that went on for some time, or was done several times. The translation *was/were* . . . is often appropriate, but with some verbs a simple past tense sounds better in English:

> illum equum decem annos habebam.
> I had (*not* was having) that horse for ten years.

• For the imperfect passive see page 93, and for the imperfect subjunctive see pages 138–9.

Exercise 25   Imperfect tense

1 senex nos de periculo viae saepe monebat.
2 multos annos Romae habitabamus.
3 hic servus semper bene laborabat.
4 quid legebas?
5 multis post diebus mari tandem appropinquabamus.
6 milites capti pro vita sua diu orabant.
7 naves Romanorum trans mare lente navigabant.
8 tres dies in castris manebamus; deinde hostes conspeximus.
9 urbem hostium decem annos oppugnabamus.
10 ubi montem ascendebam, flumen subito conspexi.

FUTURE TENSE

		I shall carry	I shall warn	I shall drag	I shall hear
sg	1	port-a-bo	mon-e-bo	trah-am	aud-i-am
	2	port-a-bis	mon-e-bis	trah-es	aud-i-es
	3	port-a-bit	*etc*	trah-et	*etc*
pl	1	port-a-bimus		trah-emus	
	2	port-a-bitis		trah-etis	
	3	port-a-bunt		trah-ent	

Note the two different patterns here. In the imperfect tense all four conjugations use the endings *-bam*, *-bas*, *-bat* etc after their characteristic vowel(s). In the future tense the first and second conjugations do something similar, with the *-bo*, *-bis*, *-bit* endings. You might expect the third and fourth to follow suit, but in fact they use the endings *-am*, *-es*, *-et* etc instead (fourth, and mixed third/fourth, with *i* in front).

The future endings for third conjugation are (except in the first person singular) the same as the present tense endings for second conjugation (*-eo*, *-es*, *-et* etc), so there is a risk of confusion unless you know or look up which conjugation a verb belongs to. Note that in a typical passage (with a story set in the past) the future tense is most likely to be met within direct speech.

• For the future passive see page 94, for the future participle see pages 126–7, and for the future infinitive see page 134.

• For the *hidden future* in time and conditional clauses see pages 111 and 114.

Exercise 26 Future tense

1 omnes liberi regem salutabunt.
2 quid nunc dicam?
3 servi vinum omnibus mox offerent.
4 hostes numquam muros nostros delebunt.
5 multa templa Romae videbimus.
6 quid in nova taberna vendes?
7 urbem nostram semper defendemus.
8 nonne hunc servum fortem liberabis?
9 cenam mox parabo.
10 quam diu dormient hi liberi?

INFINITIVE

to carry	to warn	to drag	to hear
port-are	mon-ere	trah-ere	aud-ire

The infinitive expresses the basic meaning of the verb: *to do X*. Its name indicates that it is not made *finite* (= restricted) by a person ending. It does however have a tense. This standard infinitive is the *present active* one. There are also perfect and future infinitives, and passive ones: see pages 98 and 133–4.

Note again (with slight variation from the pattern in the imperfect tense: see page 71) the use of a characteristic vowel for each conjugation, before the *-re*:

first   a
second   e (*long as in* they)
third   e (*short as in* get)
fourth   i

• Note that in the fourth conjugation the characteristic vowel is here *-i-* alone, rather than the combination *-ie-* used for other purposes (see pages 71, 118–19 and 142).

The infinitive can sometimes be translated like a noun:

amo currere.
I like running (*literally* I like to run).

Here *running* means *the act of running* (and so is different from the present participle which is an adjective and means *while running*: see pages 118–20).

Exercise 27   Infinitive

1   servum laborare iubebo.
2   num in silva diu manere times?
3   difficile erat nobis verba nuntii audire.
4   pecuniam mihi reddere debes.
5   clamores nostri equos hostium terrere possunt.

THE VERB *TO BE*

PRESENT TENSE			
			I am
sg	1		sum
	2		es
	3		est
pl	1		sumus
	2		estis
	3		sunt

- Note the similarity to French here (*je suis, tu es, il est* etc).

IMPERFECT TENSE			
			I was
sg	1		eram
	2		eras
	3		erat
pl	1		eramus
	2		eratis
	3		erant

- Note that although this does not use the *-b-* (*-bam* etc) which usually marks the imperfect tense (see page 71), the last part of each ending is still the same.

FUTURE TENSE			
			I shall be
sg	1		ero
	2		eris
	3		erit
pl	1		erimus
	2		eritis
	3		erunt

• Note that these tenses of *to be* also have other jobs in Latin. The imperfect is used as a *set of endings* to form the pluperfect of regular verbs: see page 83. The present and imperfect are used as *auxiliary verbs* to form the perfect and pluperfect passive: see pages 96–7.

The verb *to be* takes a *complement* (another noun in the nominative), not an object.

> senex olim miles erat.
> The old man was once a soldier.

Contrast this with:

> senex militem salutavit.
> The old man greeted the soldier.

The verb *to be* can come anywhere in a sentence (it does not have the same preference as other verbs for coming at the end, though it can). If it comes at the beginning of a sentence it is usually translated *there is* etc:

> est taberna in illa via.
> There is a shop in that street.

The infinitive of *sum* is *esse* (= to be).

> volo civis Romanus esse.
> I want to be a Roman citizen.

• Note that the verbs *adsum* (= I am here) and *absum* (= I am away) are *compounds* (see page 64) of *to be* and form their tenses in the same way. The verb *possum* (= I am able) is also a compound of *sum* (see page 85).

• For the perfect tense *fui* (and pluperfect *fueram*) see pages 81 and 83.

Exercise 28   The verb *to be*

1   dux noster saevissimus est.
2   illa domus est nostra.
3   num ibi semper tristis eras?
4   est equus in horto.
5   labor difficillimus erat.

PRINCIPAL PARTS

This is a system for giving important parts of a verb, from which all other information about it can be worked out. For a regular active verb there are four:

present tense (first person singular)	(see page 70)
infinitive	(see page 74)
perfect tense (first person singular)	(see page 78)
perfect passive participle* (masculine nominative singular)	(see page 121)

* In older and in more advanced books, the fourth principal part is given in a form called the *supine*, which ends *-um* like the *neuter* of the perfect passive participle.

Verbs are commonly quoted with their principal parts in the form:

porto, portare, portavi, portatus   I carry

From this you can tell that the other parts are *to carry, I (have) carried, having been carried*. With regular forms, the principal parts are often abbreviated:

porto, -are, -avi, -atus

As usual with abbreviated Latin words, you remove the last syllable of the first form quoted, then add the alternative endings.

Some verbs do not have the fourth principal part because they cannot be made passive.

• Deponent verbs (see pages 99–100) come into this category (their active perfect participle is used with the auxiliary verb *sum* as the *third* principal part).

Principal parts are a way of plotting information. If just the first person singular of the present tense were quoted, you could not tell a first conjugation verb from a third conjugation one (since both end in *-o*). If just the infinitive were quoted, you could not tell a second conjugation verb from a third conjugation one (since both end in *-ere*, though pronounced differently: see page 74). By seeing all four parts together you can work out all you need to know.

PERFECT TENSE

The word *perfect* in grammar means *completed* (rather than *faultless*: compare *imperfect*, page 71). The perfect tense refers to a completed action in the past. It has its own distinctive endings, but note that all except the first two still fit the basic pattern of person endings (see page 69). Note in particular the distinctive second person forms, both singular and plural: *-isti* and *-istis*.

sg	1	-i
	2	-isti
	3	-it
pl	1	-imus
	2	-istis
	3	-erunt

The endings themselves are the same for all four conjugations. They are added to the *perfect stem*. This is the basic verb stem added to or modified, according to conjugation. First and fourth conjugation verbs normally add a syllable with their characteristic vowel and *-v*:

	present	*perfect stem*
first conjugation	porto	portav-
fourth	audio	audiv-

Many but not all second conjugation verbs add *-u*:

second	moneo	monu-

With the third conjugation it is a bit more complicated. Many verbs add *-s* or a combination of letters involving an *s* sound, but many others are irregular (see the list on pages 80–1). As usual however the common irregular forms quickly become familiar, and looking up or learning the principal parts (see page 77) enables you to work out any perfect tense.

		I (have) carried	I (have) warned	I (have) dragged	I (have) heard
sg	1	port-av-i	mon-u-i	trax-i	aud-iv-i
	2	port-av-isti	mon-u-isti	trax-isti	aud-iv-isti
	3	port-av-it	mon-u-it	trax-it	aud-iv-it
pl	1	port-av-imus	mon-u-imus	trax-imus	aud-iv-imus
	2	port-av-istis	mon-u-istis	trax-istis	aud-iv-istis
	3	port-av-erunt	mon-u-erunt	trax-erunt	aud-iv-erunt

The perfect tense can be translated *have/has* . . . (this is sometimes called a *true* perfect, implying that the effect of the action continues):

amici nostri advenerunt et in horto sunt.
Our friends have arrived and are in the garden.

Very often however it is used as what in other languages is called a *simple past* (or *past historic* or *aorist*) for a single action, without *have* . . . in English:

amici nostri advenerunt sed mox discesserunt.
Our friends arrived but soon left.

Note that the perfect tense of the verb *to be* is *fui*. This is particularly used in the sense *used to be* (implying *but am no longer*):

servus fui sed nunc libertus sum.
I was a slave but am now a freedman.

• For *inquit* (= he said) which is present in form but usually translated like a perfect tense, and *coepi* (= I began) which is a perfect with no equivalent present tense in use, see page 90.

• For the perfect passive see page 96.

Exercise 29   Perfect tense (regular forms)

1 omnes cives ad portum festinaverunt.
2 urbem hostium tandem oppugnavimus.
3 puer epistulam in villa celavit.
4 quo heri navigavistis, nautae?
5 nuntius nos de periculo monuit.
6 novam ancillam salutavi.
7 magnam domum aedificavi et Romae nunc habito.
8 quis hos muros aedificavit?
9 custodes qui aderant nihil audiverunt.
10 cur hunc servum liberavisti, domine?

COMMON IRREGULAR
PERFECT TENSES

Here are forty-five of the most important irregular perfect tenses, which should be learned (others can be found in the vocabulary, pages 184–98):

conjugation	verb	perfect tense	meaning
1st	do	dedi	I gave
	sto	steti	I stood
2nd	iubeo	iussi	I ordered
	maneo	mansi	I remained, I stayed
	persuadeo	persuasi	I persuaded
	rideo	risi	I laughed
	sedeo	sedi	I sat
	video	vidi	I saw
3rd	ago	egi	I did, I acted
	cado	cecidi	I fell
	cognosco	cognovi	I found out
	cogo	coegi	I forced
	credo	credidi	I believed, I trusted
	curro	cucurri	I ran
	dico	dixi	I said
	discedo	discessi	I departed, I left
	duco	duxi	I led
	intellego	intellexi	I understood
	lego	legi	I read
	mitto	misi	I sent
	peto	petivi	I sought, I asked for
	pono	posui	I placed, I put
	promitto	promisi	I promised
	quaero	quaesivi	I searched for, I asked for
	rego	rexi	I ruled
	relinquo	reliqui	I left
	rumpo	rupi	I broke, I burst
	scribo	scripsi	I wrote
	surgo	surrexi	I got up
	tollo	sustuli	I raised, I lifted

conjugation	verb	perfect tense	meaning
3rd	trado	tradidi	I handed over
	traho	traxi	I dragged
	vinco	vici	I conquered, I won
	vivo	vixi	I lived
3rd/4th	accipio	accepi	I received
	capio	cepi	I took, I captured
	conspicio	conspexi	I caught sight of
	facio	feci	I made, I did
	fugio	fugi	I ran away, I fled
	iacio	ieci	I threw
4th	venio	veni	I came
Irregular	eo	i(v)i	I went
	fero	tuli	I carried, I brought
	possum	potui	I was able
	sum	fui	I was

If you note certain patterns in the list of irregular perfect tenses, they are easier to learn.

(1) Change of vowel from present stem, especially *a* to *e*:

ago	egi
capio	cepi
facio	feci
iacio	ieci

(2) Adding an *s*, which involves *c* plus *s* being written as *x*, or other similar modification to make the perfect easier to pronounce:

dico	dixi
duco	duxi
intellego	intellexi
mitto	misi
rego	rexi
scribo	scripsi

A compound verb (see pages 64–5) forms its perfect tense in the same way as the ordinary verb from which it is made:

erumpo	erupi
invenio	inveni

Exercise 30   Irregular perfect tenses (i)

1   omnes cives statim surrexerunt.
2   imperator milites in magnum periculum duxit.
3   quis hanc epistulam scripsit?
4   nuntius regis nihil mihi dixit.
5   multa dona illi seni misimus.
6   quot libros huic puero dedisti?
7   dux hostium statim discessit.
8   nautae navem in mare traxerunt.
9   quid in bello egisti, pater?
10 pueri per viam celeriter cucurrerunt.

Exercise 31   Irregular perfect tenses (ii)

1   servumne in via conspexisti?
2   nauta in mare cecidit.
3   puellae omnes riserunt.
4   miles gladios in castra tulit.
5   quis primus in summo monte stetit?
6   femina pecuniam in templo posuit.
7   ille puer nihil dicere potuit.
8   novum consilium quaesivi.
9   dominus servos laborare coegit.
10 puer portam horti rupit.

PLUPERFECT TENSE

		I had carried	I had warned	I had dragged	I had heard
sg	1	port-av-eram	mon-u-eram	trax-eram	aud-iv-eram
	2	port-av-eras	mon-u-eras	trax-eras	aud-iv-eras
	3	port-av-erat	etc	etc	etc
pl	1	port-av-eramus			
	2	port-av-eratis			
	3	port-av-erant			

The perfect stem (see page 78) is used again here. It is followed by the imperfect tense of the verb *to be* (see page 75) used as a set of endings.

Pluperfect literally means *more than perfect*: it refers to something that *had already* happened at a point in the past referred to by a perfect or imperfect tense.

> senex, qui nihil antea audiverat, epistulam brevem accepit.
> The old man, who had heard nothing previously, received a short letter.

The pluperfect refers to something two stages back: if you think of time like a lift in a multi-storey building, the pluperfect is two floors down from the present tense. The translation *had* is always used in English.

Failure to recognise and correctly translate verbs in the pluperfect tense is a very common mistake in GCSE.

- Note that the pluperfect of the verb *to be* is *fueram* (= I had been).

- For the pluperfect passive see page 96, and for the pluperfect subjunctive see page 150.

Exercise 32   Pluperfect tense

 1   librum quem olim legeram iterum inveni.
 2   militem fortiorem numquam videram.
 3   dominus servum qui multos cives servaverat libenter liberavit.
 4   senator qui surrexerat iterum sedere constituit.
 5   quid ante bellum feceras?
 6   senex illum cibum consumpserat; postea mortuus est.
 7   Romani ante illud tempus reges habuerant.
 8   ei qui nihil audiverant nihil intellegebant.
 9   miles qui montem ascenderat praemium accepit.
10   puer tandem opus fecit quod olim promiserat.

VERY IRREGULAR VERBS

		PRESENT	IMPERFECT	FUTURE	PERFECT
		I am able, I can	I was able, I could	I shall be able	I was/have been able, I could
sg	*1*	pos-sum	pot-eram	pot-ero	potu-i
	2	pot-es	pot-eras	pot-eris	potu-isti
	3	pot-est	*etc*	*etc*	*etc*
pl	*1*	pos-sumus			
	2	pot-estis			
	3	pos-sunt			

This is a compound of the verb *to be* (see page 75). It is formed by sticking *pot-* (originally a separate adjective *potis* = able) on the front of the equivalent part of *to be*. Where that starts with *s*, *pot-* changes to *pos-* (producing *ss*) to make it easier to pronounce. In the perfect tense the *f* of *fui* (the perfect of *to be*) disappears for the same reason, so *pot-fui* becomes *potui*. Similarly the pluperfect is *potueram* (= I had been able).

The verb *possum* is commonly followed by an infinitive:

hi liberi bene legere possunt.
These children can read well.

The infinitive of possum is *posse* (= to be able).

- For the imperfect and pluperfect subjunctive of *possum* see pages 138 and 150.

		PRESENT	IMPERFECT	FUTURE	PERFECT
		I go	I was going	I shall go	I went, I have gone
sg	*1*	eo	ibam	ibo	i(v)i
	2	is	ibas	ibis	i(v)isti
	3	it	ibat	ibit	i(v)it
pl	*1*	imus	ibamus	ibimus	i(v)imus
	2	itis	ibatis	ibitis	istis *or* ivistis
	3	eunt	ibant	ibunt	i(v)erunt

Note here the similarity to equivalent tenses of regular verbs: the present tense is almost the same as the endings for third conjugation (see page 70), the imperfect and future endings are abbreviated versions of regular patterns (see pages 71 and 73), and the perfect tense has regular perfect endings on a perfect stem, which can be either *i*- or *iv*- for the perfect tense itself, but is just *i*- in the pluperfect *ieram* (= I had gone).

The infinitive of *eo* is *ire* (= to go).

Exercise 33   Very irregular verbs (i)

1 haec verba facile legere possum.
2 quo nunc itis, pueri?
3 frater meus celeriter currere potest.
4 ubi domum ibam clamorem subito audivi.
5 nihil antea intellegere potueram; deinde hunc librum inveni.
6 ubi Romam iero imperatorem salutabo.
7 omnes hi milites fortiter pugnare poterant.
8 in forum mox ibimus.
9 quis in hac insula habitare potest?
10 nemo pecuniam invenire potuit.

The following three verbs should be studied together, noting recurrent features.

		PRESENT	IMPERFECT	FUTURE	PERFECT
		I want	I wanted, I was wanting	I shall want	I (have) wanted
sg	1	volo	volebam	volam	volui
	2	vis	volebas	voles	voluisti
	3	vult	*etc*	*etc*	*etc*
pl	1	volumus			
	2	vultis			
	3	volunt			
infinitive: velle				*pluperfect:* volueram, volueras *etc*	

This is a modified version of third conjugation (in some bits of the present, in the imperfect and in the future: see pages 70–1 and 73), though its perfect stem is more like second conjugation (see pages 78–9).

	PRESENT	IMPERFECT	FUTURE	PERFECT
	I do not want	I did not want	I shall not want	I did not want, I have not wanted
sg 1	nolo	nolebam	nolam	nolui
2	non vis	nolebas	noles	noluisti
3	non vult	*etc*	*etc*	*etc*
pl 1	nolumus			
2	non vultis			
3	nolunt			

infinitive: nolle   *pluperfect:* nolueram, nolueras *etc*

This is a compound (see page 64) of *volo*, using the negative *non* (= not) as a prefix. When *non* is stuck on the front of *vol-* it shortens to *nol-*. The same thing does not happen with the irregular bits starting *vu-* or *vi-*, so some bits of the present tense stay as two separate words.

- For the use of the imperative of *nolo* (*noli, nolite*) in a negative direct command see page 102.

	PRESENT	IMPERFECT	FUTURE	PERFECT
	I prefer	I was preferring	I shall prefer	I (have) preferred
sg 1	malo	malebam	malam	malui
2	mavis	malebas	males	maluisti
3	mavult	*etc*	*etc*	*etc*
pl 1	malumus			
2	mavultis			
3	malunt			

infinitive: malle   *pluperfect:* malueram, malueras *etc*

This too is a compound of *volo*, using a shortened form of the comparative adverb *magis* (= more) as a prefix: it means *want* something *more* than something else.

Finally under the heading of irregular verbs note *fero*, which is basically third conjugation but loses some vowels from its endings and has unusual principal parts:

fero, ferre, tuli, latus

PRESENT		ACTIVE	PASSIVE
		I carry	I am carried
sg	*1*	fero	feror
	2	fers	fer(e)ris
	3	fert	fertur
pl	*1*	ferimus	ferimur
	2	fertis	ferimini
	3	ferunt	feruntur
imperative:		fer (see page 102), ferte	
imperfect:		ferebam, ferebas *etc*	
future:		feram, feres *etc*	
perfect:		tuli, tulisti *etc*	
perfect passive:		latus sum, latus es *etc*	

• The following verbs are compounds (see page 64) of *fero*, with similar principal parts:

aufero, auferre, abstuli, ablatus	I take away, I steal	(*au* = *ab*, away)
offero, offerre, obtuli, oblatus	I offer	(*ob* = for)

• Note also that the last two parts are found with the prefix *sub-* as the last two principal parts of *tollo*, formed as if it had started *subfero* (which would have the same meaning):

tollo, tollere, sustuli, sublatus   I raise, I lift up

Exercise 34   Very irregular verbs (ii)

1   hic senex epistulam accipere vult.
2   mater mea heri exire nolebat.
3   nemo hunc senatorem audire volebat.
4   servus mihi cibum tulit quem consumere antea nolueram.
5   cur respondere non vis?
6   facilius est velle quam facere.
7   malumus in villa manere quam ad urbem ambulare.
8   quis hunc librum legere volet?
9   quid in villam fertis, servi?
10 cur hic sedere mavis?

DEFECTIVE VERBS

A *defective* verb is one of which only a few bits exist.

(1) A very common example is *inquit* (= he/she says/said). It is normally found only in this third person form (though there is a plural *inquiunt* = they say/said). It is in origin a present tense but is usually translated like a perfect. It is used to quote the actual words of a speaker, which it often interrupts:

> 'ecce' inquit 'amici nostri appropinquant.'
> 'Look!' he said 'our friends are approaching.'

In this example it is effective to keep the same order in English, with *he said* interrupting the quotation. Often however it is better translated first, especially if a subject is given:

> nuntius 'festinate, cives,' inquit 'nam hostes urbi appropinquant.'
> The messenger said 'Hurry, citizens, for the enemy are approaching the city.'

• Note carefully that *inquit* means *said* (not *asked*): this is a common mistake in GCSE. The word may coincidentally be used with a question, but it has no connection with the English *inquire*.

(2) The following verb exists only in perfect tense forms (and the associated pluperfect), but with all three persons, singular and plural:

	coepi	I have begun, I began	(see page 78)
	coeperam	I had begun	(see page 83)
infinitive	coepisse	to have begun	(like a perfect infinitive: page 133)

Exercise 35 Defective verbs

1 heri librum longum legere coepi.
2 puella 'numquam' inquit 'pueris iterum credam.'
3 prima luce profecti sumus, sed hostes antea fugere coeperant.
4 servus 'haec' inquit 'est domus consulis.'
5 coepistine haec verba intellegere?

ACTIVE AND PASSIVE

With an active verb the grammatical subject is also the person or thing who does the action:

The boy *kicks* the ball.

With a passive verb the grammatical subject is on the receiving end of the action:

The ball *is kicked* by the boy.

Passive verbs in Latin are easy to recognise. Most present, imperfect and future active forms can be converted to their passive equivalents by a simple formula. Here are the basic person endings for each:

		active	*passive*
sg	*1*	-o *or* -m	-r (*added to* -o, *or in place of* -m)
	2	-s	-ris
	3	-t	-tur
pl	*1*	-mus	-mur
	2	-tis	-mini
	3	-nt	-ntur

The vowel(s) in front of these person endings will usually be the same as in the active. This formula works for the present, imperfect and future tenses. Here are some examples:

present
   portas   you (*sg*) carry
   portaris   you (*sg*) are being carried

imperfect
   monebamus   we were warning
   monebamur   we were being warned

future
   audient   they will hear
   audientur   they will be heard

• The only minor exception to note is that the second person singular of the present tense of third conjugation, and of the future tense of first and second conjugations, is -*eris* in the passive instead of the expected -*iris*:

| mittis | you (*sg*) send |
| mitteris | you (*sg*) are sent |

| videbis | you (*sg*) will see |
| videberis | you (*sg*) will be seen |

• This formula also works for the passive form of the imperfect subjunctive: see page 139.

• The perfect and pluperfect passive are formed in a different way: see page 96.

PRESENT, IMPERFECT AND FUTURE PASSIVE

<table>
<tr><td colspan="6">PRESENT PASSIVE</td></tr>
<tr><td></td><td></td><td>I am carried</td><td>I am warned</td><td>I am dragged</td><td>I am heard</td></tr>
<tr><td>sg</td><td>1</td><td>portor</td><td>moneor</td><td>trahor</td><td>audior</td></tr>
<tr><td></td><td>2</td><td>portaris</td><td>moneris</td><td>traheris*</td><td>audiris</td></tr>
<tr><td></td><td>3</td><td>portatur</td><td>monetur</td><td>trahitur</td><td>auditur</td></tr>
<tr><td>pl</td><td>1</td><td>portamur</td><td>monemur</td><td>trahimur</td><td>audimur</td></tr>
<tr><td></td><td>2</td><td>portamini</td><td>monemini</td><td>trahimini</td><td>audimini</td></tr>
<tr><td></td><td>3</td><td>portantur</td><td>monentur</td><td>trahuntur</td><td>audiuntur</td></tr>
</table>

* Note the ending *-eris* instead of the expected *-iris*: see pages 91–2.

The present passive can be translated *I am being carried* (implying *at this moment*), as well as *I am carried*.

<table>
<tr><td colspan="6">IMPERFECT PASSIVE</td></tr>
<tr><td></td><td></td><td>I was being carried</td><td>I was being warned</td><td>I was being dragged</td><td>I was being heard</td></tr>
<tr><td>sg</td><td>1</td><td>portabar</td><td>monebar</td><td>trahebar</td><td>audiebar</td></tr>
<tr><td></td><td>2</td><td>portabaris</td><td>monebaris</td><td>trahebaris</td><td>audiebaris</td></tr>
<tr><td></td><td>3</td><td>portabatur</td><td>*etc*</td><td>*etc*</td><td>*etc*</td></tr>
<tr><td>pl</td><td>1</td><td>portabamur</td><td></td><td></td><td></td></tr>
<tr><td></td><td>2</td><td>portabamini</td><td></td><td></td><td></td></tr>
<tr><td></td><td>3</td><td>portabantur</td><td></td><td></td><td></td></tr>
</table>

FUTURE PASSIVE

		I shall be carried	I shall be warned	I shall be dragged	I shall be heard
sg	1	portabor	monebor	trahar	audiar
	2	portaberis*	moneberis*	traheris	audieris
	3	portabitur	*etc*	trahetur	*etc*
pl	1	portabimur		trahemur	
	2	portabimini		trahemini	
	3	portabuntur		trahentur	

As with the future active (page 73), note the distinction between two sets of endings: a passive version of *-bo*, *-bis*, *-bit* for first and second conjugations, and a passive version of *-am*, *-es*, *-et* for third and fourth.

* Note the ending *-eris* instead of the expected *-iris*: see pages 91–2.

AGENT AND INSTRUMENT

Consider the following simple sentence (consisting of subject, object and active verb):

servus dominum necat.
The slave kills the master.

When this is made passive, the original object becomes the subject, and the original subject becomes the *agent* (the *person by whom* the action is done), expressed by *a* (or *ab* if the next word starts with a vowel or *h*-) and the ablative:

dominus a servo necatur.
The master is killed by the slave.

If with a passive verb we are told the *thing with which* the action is done, this is called the *instrument* and is also put in the ablative, but without *a/ab*:

dominus gladio necatur.
The master is killed with a sword.

Both agent and instrument can be expressed in the same sentence:

dominus a servo gladio necatur.
The master is killed by the slave with a sword.

Exercise 36   Present, imperfect and future passive; agent and instrument

1   cibus a pueris consumebatur.
2   hic liber saepe legitur.
3   villa nova mox hic aedificabitur.
4   cur a domino laudabaris?
5   omnes cives clamoribus hostium terrentur.
6   multae epistulae mihi a matre mittebantur.
7   murus ab hostibus nunc deletur.
8   equi in castra a servis ducebantur.
9   vox regis numquam iterum audietur.
10   haec urbs decem annos oppugnabatur.

PERFECT AND PLUPERFECT PASSIVE

PERFECT PASSIVE

		I was/have been carried	I was/have been warned	I was/have been dragged	I was/have been heard
sg	1	portatus sum	monitus sum	tractus sum	auditus sum
	2	portatus es	monitus es	tractus es	auditus es
	3	portatus est	*etc*	*etc*	*etc*
pl	1	portati sumus			
	2	portati estis			
	3	portati sunt			

The perfect passive is made up of the *perfect passive participle* (see page 121) with the *present* tense of the verb *to be* (see page 75) used as an auxiliary verb. The present is used because the participle is perfect tense already. The perfect passive literally means *I am in a state of having been carried*, i.e. *I have been carried* or simply *I was carried*. Note that the participle is always nominative, but changes its ending according to the number and gender of the subject.

PLUPERFECT PASSIVE

		I had been carried	I had been warned	I had been dragged	I had been heard
sg	1	portatus eram	monitus eram	tractus eram	auditus eram
	2	portatus eras	monitus eras	tractus eras	auditus eras
	3	portatus erat	*etc*	*etc*	*etc*
pl	1	portati eramus			
	2	portati eratis			
	3	portati erant			

The pluperfect passive is formed in a comparable way. Here the auxiliary verb is the *imperfect* tense of the verb *to be* (see page 75): added to the participle which is perfect tense already, it creates the pluperfect, which is two stages back (see page 83). The pluperfect passive literally means *I was* (already, at some time in the past) *in a state of having been carried*, i.e. *I had been carried*.

Exercise 37   Perfect and pluperfect passive

1 servus fortissimus a domino liberatus est.
2 milites qui a rege ducti erant omnes postea effugerunt.
3 multa pecunia huic servo data est.
4 dux hostium tandem occisus est.
5 novum consilium a captivis celeriter factum est.
6 clamor a puella auditus erat, sed nihil aliud cognovimus.
7 pueri domum redire iussi sunt.
8 cena optima nobis a matre parata est.
9 epistula mihi a sorore antea missa erat.
10 verba quae a liberto dicta erant ab omnibus laudata sunt.

PASSIVE INFINITIVE

The forms of the present *active* infinitive (see page 74) for the four conjugations are:

to carry	to warn	to drag	to hear
port-are	mon-ere	trah-ere	aud-ire

These are made *passive* by changing the final *-e* to *-i*, except that in the third conjugation the *-er-* drops out, so that the passive infinitive ending is just *-i*:

to be carried	to be warned	to be dragged	to be heard
port-ari	mon-eri	trah-i	aud-iri

• Note carefully this unusual formation for the third conjugation, since with some verbs it may look like the first person singular of the perfect tense (e.g. *legi* = to be read *or* I have read), or like the dative singular of a related third declension noun: e.g. *rego* (= I rule) has passive infinitive *regi* (= to be ruled), which is the same as the dative of *rex* (= king).

• For further infinitives (perfect active and passive, and future active) see pages 133–4.

• For the use of any type of infinitive in indirect statement see pages 132–7.

Exercise 38   Passive infinitive

1   num hic cibus consumi potest?
2   haec puella a te amari non vult.
3   epistula quam scripsisti statim mitti debet.
4   nonne hi clamores ab omnibus audiri possunt?
5   iubeo omnes servos meos nunc liberari.

DEPONENT VERBS

Deponent verbs are *passive* in form but *active* in meaning: they look as if they are passive, but are actually active (the term *deponent* is not very informative: it literally means *laying aside*, i.e. *not taking up* a passive sense). They are formed like the passive equivalent of each tense, according to their conjugation. Their principal parts (see page 77) therefore look like this:

conor, conari, conatus sum I try

A deponent verb behaves in a sentence just like an ordinary active one. (Note however that it cannot be *made* passive: it has *only* a passive *form*, but *only* an active *meaning*.)

conjugation	1st	2nd	3rd
	I try	I seem	I speak
(like present, imperfect and future passive: see pages 93–4)			
present	conor	videor	loquor
imperfect	conabar	videbar	loquebar
future	conabor	videbor	loquar
(like perfect and pluperfect passive: see page 96)			
perfect	conatus sum	visus sum	locutus sum
pluperfect	conatus eram	visus eram	locutus eram
(like passive infinitive: see page 98)			
infinitive	conari	videri	loqui

Other deponent verbs:

hortor, hortari, hortatus sum	I encourage, I urge
in/e/re-gredior, -gredi, -gressus sum	I go in/out/back (*also* progredior = I advance)
miror, mirari, miratus sum	I wonder at, I admire
morior, mori, mortuus sum	I die
patior, pati, passus sum	I suffer, I endure
precor, precari, precatus sum	I pray (to)
proficiscor, proficisci, profectus sum	I set out
sequor, sequi, secutus sum	I follow

The perfect participle with active meaning (e.g. *locutus* = having spoken) is a useful feature of deponent verbs that does not exist in Latin otherwise. Sometimes it is better translated like a present (e.g. *miratus* = wondering at): this must be judged from the context. Deponent verbs also have a present active participle of regular form (e.g. *moriens* = dying): see pages 118–19.

Exercise 39   Deponent verbs

1   haec verba legere diu conabar.
2   imperator milites suos breviter hortatus est.
3   ille senator semper optime loquitur.
4   frater huius senis mortuus est.
5   prima luce e castris profecti sumus.
6   servus fugit sed custodes celeriter sequebantur.
7   quid tum loquebaris, fili?
8   equus in hortum villae ingressus est.
9   nos omnes vulnera gravissima passi sumus.
10   nuntius mox regredietur.

SEMI-DEPONENT VERBS

There are only a few of these. They are active in form in the present, imperfect and future tenses, but become deponent (using the passive forms) in the perfect, pluperfect and future perfect.

			I rejoice
			(2nd)
PRESENT			
sg	1		gaudeo
	2		gaudes
	3		gaudet
pl	1		gaudemus
	2		gaudetis
	3		gaudent
imperfect			gaudebam
future			gaudebo
(like perfect and pluperfect passive: see page 96)			
perfect			gavisus sum
pluperfect			gavisus eram

Similarly:

audeo, audere, ausus sum	I dare
soleo, solere, solitus sum	I am accustomed

All three semi-deponent verbs needed for GCSE are second conjugation.

- It is important not to confuse *audeo* with *audio* (= I hear): see page 164.

Exercise 40   Semi-deponent verbs

1   puella ubi verba nuntii audivit maxime gavisa est.
2   ille puer celeriter currere solebat.
3   post bellum omnes gaudebimus.
4   ego hoc legere numquam ausus sum.
5   quamquam talia facere numquam solitus erat, servus cibum abstulit.

DIRECT COMMANDS

A direct command, telling someone to do something, is expressed by a form of the verb called the *imperative* (from *impero* = I order):

	carry!	warn!	drag!	listen!
sg	port-a	mon-e	trah-e	aud-i
pl	port-ate	mon-ete!	trah-ite!	aud-ite!

Note that the imperative endings for each conjugation use the same vowel as the infinitive (see page 74), except that the third conjugation has *-ite* in the plural.

• Four common third conjugation (or related irregular) verbs drop the *-e* ending in the singular:

dic	say! speak! tell!
duc	lead!
fer	carry!
fac	make! do!

A negative direct command, telling someone *not* to do something, is expressed in a distinctive way. It does not (as you might expect) use a negative with the imperative, but uses the imperative of the irregular verb *nolo* (= I do not want, I am unwilling: see page 87) as a sort of auxiliary verb:

	sg	*pl*
imperatives of nolo:	noli	nolite

This is followed by the *infinitive* of the verb expressing what is not to be done:

negative command:	noli festinare nolite festinare
literally	Be unwilling to hurry!
i.e.	Do not hurry!

• An imperative is often found with a vocative: see page 4.

• For indirect or reported commands (e.g. *I told him to go away*) see pages 144–5.

Exercise 41   Direct commands

1 da mihi illam pecuniam, serve!
2 tacete omnes!
3 urbem fortiter defendite, milites!
4 eicite hos pueros!
5 noli auxilium talibus hominibus dare!
6 vende hunc equum, domine!
7 duc me ad ducem tuum!
8 in forum festinate, cives!
9 nolite domi narrare verba quae hic audivistis!
10 cibum fer! cenam fac!

DIRECT QUESTIONS

A direct question, like a direct command, quotes the actual words of a speaker and it ends with a question mark. It is important to distinguish two basic types:

(1) Questions asking if something is the case, to which the answer will be *Yes* or *No*.

Any sentence can be made into a question by adding a question mark:

> equum habes?
> Do you have a horse?

More commonly the question is signalled by adding *-ne* to the end of the first word:

> equumne habes?

• Compare how *-que* (= and) is similarly added to the end of another word (see page 66). Adding *-ne* may make a familiar word look strange:

> tene ibi vidi?
> Did I see you there?

• This *-ne* must be carefully distinguished from the negative *ne* (= not, so as not to): see page 157.

A question can be slanted to suggest that the speaker expects or hopes for a particular answer by using *nonne* (*non* plus *ne*: *literally* is it not the case that? i.e. surely?) or *num* (surely . . . not?):

	nonne equum habes?	
	Surely you have a horse?	
or	Don't you have a horse?	(*expecting* Yes)
	num equum habes?	
	Surely you don't have a horse?	(*expecting* No)

• This use of *num* must be carefully distinguished from its use to mean *whether* in an indirect question (see pages 154–5 and 162).

Exercise 42   Direct questions (with *ne, nonne, num*)

1   regemne vidisti?
2   nonne hoc iter difficile erit?
3   num totum diem dormiebas?
4   gladium habes?
5   gravissimumne est vulnus imperatoris?
6   nonne hunc librum legistis, pueri?
7   tune clamorem audivisti?
8   num talem cibum amas?
9   servine estis?
10   nonne navem conspexistis, cives?

(2) A question asking for specific information is introduced by one of the following question words:

cur	why?
quam	how?
quando	when?
quomodo	how? in what way?
ubi	where?
quo	where to?
unde	where from?
quis, quid	who? which? what?
quantus -a -um	how big?
quot	how many?
qualis -e	what sort of?

Note how most of these begin *qu-* (and an older spelling of *cur* was *quor*): this corresponds to the *wh-* of many equivalent words in English.

Most of these words are adverbs (*quomodo* is originally an ablative phrase *quo modo*, made into one word and used as an adverb). See page 57 for declension of the pronoun *quis, quid*. The last three are adjectives: *quantus* is regular 2-1-2 in declension (see page 24), *quot* is indeclinable, and *qualis* is third declension like *fortis* (see page 25).

Because the question word normally starts the sentence, the subject is postponed:

quid dixit rex?
What did the king say?

- Note carefully the distinction between the plural of *quantus*, and *quot*:

> quantas naves habetis?
> What size of ships do you have?

> quot naves habetis?
> How many ships do you have?

- Note that *quam* can also introduce an *exclamation*:

> quam fortis es.
> How brave you are!

- Some of the words which introduce questions are also used in other contexts:

> rediimus in castra unde profecti eramus.
> We returned to the camp from where we had set out.

Note in particular *ubi*: in a question it always means *where*, but elsewhere can mean either *where* or *when* (introducing a time clause: see page 111):

> locum quaerebam ubi haec acciderunt.
> I was looking for the place where these things happened.

> ubi locum inveni, magnopere gavisus sum.
> When I found the place, I was very pleased.

Exercise 43 Direct questions (asking for specific information)

1 cur tam diu aberatis, amici?
2 quem in horto heri vidisti, senex?
3 quo festinatis, cives?
4 ubi sunt feminae quas custodiebas?
5 unde profecti sunt amici nostri? quando advenient?
6 quid in illa urbe post bellum accidit?
7 quot servos habes, et quantam villam?
8 qualem cibum mavis?
9 quis necavit militem qui nos servaverat?
10 quomodo hoc facere poterimus?

NUMERALS

unus, una, unum	one
duo, duae, duo	two
tres, tria	three
quattuor	four
quinque	five
sex	six
septem	seven
octo	eight
novem	nine
decem	ten
centum	100
mille, *pl* milia	1000

Note also the following adjective (regular 2-1-2 in declension: see page 24):

primus -a -um   first

Numbers above three are indeclinable, except that *mille* has a plural. Declensions of the small numbers are:

	one		
	m	*f*	*n*
nom	unus	una	unum
acc	unum	unam	unum
gen	unius	unius	unius
dat	uni	uni	uni
abl	uno	una	uno

(*unus* is modifed 2-1-2, with genitive and dative like a pronoun: see pages 24 and 43)

	two		
	m	*f*	*n*
nom	duo	duae	duo
acc	duos	duas	duo
gen	duorum	duarum	duorum
dat	duobus	duabus	duobus
abl	duobus	duabus	duobus

	three	
	m/f	*n*
nom	tres	tria
acc	tres	tria
gen	trium	trium
dat	tribus	tribus
abl	tribus	tribus

Exercise 44   Numerals

1   mille milites quinque annos fortiter pugnabant.
2   dominus cum tribus ancillis Romam iter fecit.
3   frater meus centum libros habet.
4   senex duorum filiorum pater est.
5   pedes unius equi vulnerati erant.

TIME EXPRESSIONS

Time *how long* is expressed by the *accusative*:

multas horas manebamus.
We stayed for many hours.

totam noctem dormire volo.
I want to sleep for the whole night (*or* all night)

Time *when* or *within which* is expressed by the *ablative*:

Romam illo die tandem vidimus.
On that day we finally saw Rome.

milites prima luce profecti sunt.
The soldiers set out at first light (*or* at dawn).

amicus meus tribus diebus adveniet.
My friend will arrive within three days.

• Some prepositions (see page 61) are used in expressions of time:

per decem annos ibi pugnabamus.
literally   We were fighting there through ten years (i.e. for ten whole years)

Here the use of *per* is a bit more emphatic than the accusative alone.

post cenam librum legi.
After dinner I read a book.

Here *post* as usual takes the accusative. Note however:

multis post annis vicimus.
After many years we were victorious.

Here instead of *post* being a preposition with the accusative, it is used as an adverb (*literally* afterwards by many years). Except in phrases like this, the adverb is usually *postea* (see below).

Note the important distinction between:

post cenam	after dinner	*preposition*	(see page 61)
postea	afterwards	*adverb*	(see page 36)
postquam	after X *happened*, . . .	*conjunction*	(see page 66)

• The adverb *postea* is in origin *post* (the preposition) plus *ea* = these things (neuter accusative plural of *is*, *ea*, *id*: see page 43). The conjunction *postquam* means literally *after than*, and introduces a subordinate time clause (see page 111): at a later time *than* one thing happened, a second thing happened.

Exercise 45   Time expressions

1 feminae murum tres dies fortissime custodiebant.
2 novum templum illo anno aedificatum est.
3 fratres mei paucis diebus advenient.
4 Romani hostibus multos annos resistebant.
5 per totam noctem ibi manebamus; prima luce flumen transire conati sumus.
6 post mortem uxoris, senex tristis erat.
7 haec pecunia quinque annos in terra celata erat.
8 decem post annis urbem hostium tandem cepimus.
9 tribus diebus auxilium exspecto.
10 duae legiones eodem die advenerunt.

TIME CLAUSES

Clauses expressing *when* something happens are normally straightforward to translate and have an ordinary indicative verb. They are introduced by words such as:

dum	while
ubi	when
simulac (*or* simulatque)	as soon as (*literally* at the same time as)
postquam	after

• Note that *ubi* can also mean *where*, either in a question or introducing a clause stating where something happens (see pages 105–6).

• Note that *dum* can also mean *until*, if it is used with a subjunctive verb (see page 143).

To give a vivid sense of two things happening simultaneously, *dum* meaning *while* is usually followed by a present tense, translated as an imperfect if the action took place in the past:

     dum per silvam ambulo, pecuniam inveni.
lit   While I am walking through the wood, I found some money.
i.e. While I was walking through the wood, I found some money.

• This is a sort of automatic historic present (see page 70), or it could be compared to the way a present participle is used, its tense expressing relationship to that of the main verb (see page 119).

To express two things in the past that took place one after the other, *ubi* or *postquam* is usually used with a perfect tense rather than the pluperfect that might be expected (either is natural in English):

    postquam Romam adveni, domum amici quaesivi.
    After I (had) arrived in Rome, I looked for my friend's house.

• The perfect tense is used here because the thought is 'after X happened, Y happened' (rather than 'in a situation when X had happened, Y happened').

A time clause referring to the future has a *hidden future* verb (a future tense expressing accurately when the action happens, but translated in English as a present):

    ubi praemium habebo, laetus ero.
lit   When I shall have the prize, I shall be happy.
i.e. When I have the prize, I shall be happy.

• For the use of *cum* with a subjunctive verb expressing *when* with a suggestion also of *because*, see page 152.

Exercise 46   Time clauses

1   cives, simulac clamores audiverunt, in forum cucurrerunt.
2   postquam epistulam tuam accepi miserrimus eram.
3   dum per terram hostium iter facimus saevissime oppugnati sumus.
4   hic puer, ubi pecuniam inveniet, laetissimus erit.
5   ubi Romam advenio semper laetus sum.

BECAUSE AND ALTHOUGH CLAUSES

Like time clauses, these are generally straightforward to translate and have ordinary indicative verbs. They are introduced by:

quod   because
quamquam   although

Both describe circumstances and reasons: *because* gives a reason why something happens, *although* gives a reason why it might have been expected not to:

quod crudelis est, dominus a servis timetur.
Because he is cruel, the master is feared by his slaves.

quamquam crudelis est, dominus a servis amatur.
Although he is cruel, the master is loved by his slaves.

• For the various meanings of *quod* see page 162.

• For the use of *cum* with a subjunctive verb to mean *since* (strictly for a *suggested* reason, but often not much different from the use of *quod* here) see page 152.

Exercise 47   *Because* and *although* clauses

1   duci nostro credimus quod fortissimus est.
2   quamquam bene laboravi, nullum praemium accepi.
3   puer perterritus erat quod librum incenderat.
4   quod pecuniam non habeo, cibum emere non possum.
5   quamquam fortis es, hostes timere cogeris.

IF CLAUSES (CONDITIONALS)

A clause containing *si* (= if) is known as a *conditional*, because it sets a condition: if one thing is true, something else follows. Simple conditionals translate naturally into English:

>si tu laetus es, ego quoque gaudeo.
>If you are happy, I too am pleased.

A future conditional has a *hidden* future verb (a future tense translated as a present), as in a time clause (see page 111):

>si hunc librum leges, omnia intelleges.
>*lit*   If you will read this book, you will understand everything.
>*i.e.*   If you read this book, you will understand everything.

The *if* clause can come anywhere in the sentence:

>servus stultus erat si hoc fecit.
>The slave was stupid if he did this.

The other part of the sentence is typically a statement, but can be for example a command (see page 102):

>si librum meum habes, statim redde.
>If you have my book, give it back at once!

A negative conditional uses *nisi*, which can be translated either *if not* or *unless*:

>nisi librum reddes, domum incendam.
>If you do not give back the book, I will set the house on fire.
>*or*   Unless you give back the book, I will set the house on fire.

Exercise 48 *If* clauses

 1 si haec dicis, stultus es.
 2 si ad urbem venies, te libenter salutabo.
 3 si captivos necavistis, scelesti estis.
 4 si me Romam ire vis, pecuniam mitte!
 5 si bene laboratis, nos omnes gaudemus.
 6 tristis ero nisi te videbo.
 7 si puer hoc fecit, fortissimus erat.
 8 si pecuniam habes, statim mihi redde!
 9 laetus sum si cibum vinumque habeo.
10 nisi viam mox inveniam, domum redire numquam potero.

CONNECTING RELATIVE

A connecting relative is the relative pronoun (see page 54) used to start a new sentence (or a new clause after a semi-colon, which is virtually a new sentence). The appropriate translation here is not the usual *who/which* but (according to number, gender and context) for example *he, she, it, they, these things*: the trick is to identify the part of the relative pronoun that is being used, then think of and translate the equivalent bit of *is, ea, id* (see page 43) or *hic, haec, hoc* (see page 48).

> ancilla tandem advenit. quam ubi vidi, laetissimus eram.
> *lit*   The slave-girl finally arrived. Whom when I saw, I was very happy
> *i.e.*   The slave-girl finally arrived. When I saw <u>her</u>, I was very happy.

> rex nuntios misit; qui cum advenissent totam rem nobis narraverunt.
> *lit*   The king sent messengers. Who when had arrived, they told us the whole story.
> *i.e.*   The king sent messengers. When <u>they</u> had arrived, they told us the whole story.

The connecting relative is very common and it is important to be able to recognise it. It is often found as part an ablative absolute (see pages 129–31) or a *cum* clause (see page 152) beginning the new sentence. Because the relative pronoun needs to come first word in the new sentence, some adjustment of word order may be needed in English.

Particular care is needed with *quam* and *quod* because they have several different meanings (see page 162). Only context and sense enable you to tell whether *quod* starting a sentence is a connecting relative or *because* (see page 113).

Note also that *quod* as a connecting relative can be used without a particular neuter word as antecedent, instead referring more loosely to the whole of the previous sentence:

> milites nostri omnes effugerunt. quod ubi vidimus, laetissimi eramus.
> *lit*   Our soldiers all escaped. Which (thing) when we saw, we were very happy.
> *i.e.*   Our soldiers all escaped. When we saw <u>this</u>, we were very happy.

Exercise 49   Connecting relative (i)

1   hanc puellam olim cognoveram. quam heri iterum conspectam libenter salutavi.
2   nullum cibum habet hic senex; cui volo te cenam optimam parare.
3   a servo fideli servatus sum; quem postea laudatum laete liberavi.
4   imperator noster novum consilium habet. quod ubi audietis, omnes mirabimini.
5   milites fortiter pugnantes vidi. qui, postquam hostes vicerunt, ad regem misi sunt.

Exercise 50   Connecting relative (ii) (including ablative absolute or *cum* clause)

1   puer a te missus tandem advenit. cuius verbis auditis viam invenire poteramus.
2   nuntius verba imperatoris nuntiavit. quae cum audivissent, cives gavisi sunt.
3   princeps fratrem non amabat. quo postea necato, etiam crudelior erat.
4   rex militem quendam dona ferentem Romam misit. qui cum advenisset, senatoribus totam rem narravit.
5   novus imperator promisit se multa pro civibus facturum esse. quibus confectis, ab omnibus laudatus est.

PRESENT ACTIVE PARTICIPLE

A *participle* is an adjective formed from a verb. It has characteristics of both: it has endings showing number, gender and case like an adjective, and has a tense (and may have an object) like a verb.

Most Latin verbs have three participles:

present active	*e.g.*	portans	carrying
perfect passive		portatus	(having been) carried
future active		portaturus	about to carry

		carrying	
		m/f	*n*
sg	*nom*	portans	portans
	acc	portant-em	portans
	gen	portant-is	
	dat	portant-i	
	abl	portant-e*	
pl	*nom*	portant-es	portant-ia
	acc	portant-es	portant-ia
	gen	portant-ium	
	dat	portant-ibus	
	abl	portant-ibus	

*The ablative singular is -*e* in ablative absolute (see pages 129–31), but -*i* if used purely as an adjective.

The model for this is a third declension adjective like *ingens* (see page 26), using in the first part of the ending the characteristic vowel(s) for the conjugation (see page 71). Because that vowel is *e* for second and third conjugation, their present participles decline just like *ingens* (except for the variant ablative singular noted above). First conjugation has -*a*- in the first part of the ending as shown above, and fourth has -*ie*-. Thus:

		2nd	3rd	4th
		warning	dragging	hearing
		m/f	m/f	m/f
sg	nom	monens	trahens	audiens
	acc	monentem	trahentem	audientem
		etc	etc	etc

• Deponent verbs (see pages 99–100) have a present active participle of normal form, e.g. *conans* (= trying).

• Note carefully the unusual present participle of the irregular verb *eo* = I go (see pages 85–6): nominative *iens* (as you might expect), but then stem *eunt-*, so accusative singular *euntem*.

The literal translation of the present active participle is *(while) X-ing*. The tense of any participle tells us when the action happens *in relation to the main verb of the sentence*. Thus a present participle with a past main verb describes two things happening simultaneously in the past:

  exiit ridens.
  He went out laughing.

  pueros cibum consumentes vidimus.
  We saw the boys eating the food.

In these examples the translation *-ing* sounds fine in English, but often the participle is better expanded into a clause introduced by *when* or *while*. If the main verb is past (as it usually is in a passage) the present participle comes out like an imperfect tense (whose person also comes from the main verb):

  per viam ambulantes, clamorem audivimus.
  While we were walking along the road, we heard a shout.

Any participle, like any adjective, can be used as a noun (supplying from the context a word such as *people*). The present participle is often used like this in the genitive plural, and can be difficult to recognise:

  turba audientium adest.
  lit A crowd of listening ones is here.
  i.e. A crowd of listeners (*or* people listening) is here.

Exercise 51   Present active participle

1   amicos ridentes audivimus.
2   puella fugiens non visa est.
3   puerum vinum bibentem conspexi.
4   filia senis morientis miserrima est.
5   senator ad forum ambulans nihil in via vidit.
6   nautas proficiscentes hortatus sum.
7   videsne illos senes in horto sedentes?
8   clamor puerorum pugnantium saepe ibi auditur.
9   cibum militi laboranti dedi.
10 verba imperatoris animos audientium terruerunt.

PERFECT PASSIVE PARTICIPLE

This is the most common participle, and one of the most important building-blocks in Latin grammar.

		(having been) carried		
		m	*f*	*n*
sg	*nom*	portat-us	portat-a	portat-um
	acc	portat-um	portat-am	portat-um
		etc	*etc*	*etc*
		(regular 2-1-2: see page 24)		

The perfect passive participle is the fourth of the principal parts (see page 77). It may be regular or irregular in formation, according to conjugation:

first	-atus *as above*
second	*often* -itus *(like fourth), but some irregular*
third	*mostly irregular, and need to be learned*
fourth	-itus

2nd	*3rd*	*4th*
(having been)	(having been)	(having been)
warned	dragged	heard
monitus -a -um	tractus -a -um	auditus -a -um

A list of important irregular perfect passive participles is given on page 123.

• The perfect passive participle is used to form several other important pieces of grammar (see pages 96 and 133):

perfect passive	portatus sum	I was carried
pluperfect passive	portatus eram	I had been carried
perfect passive infinitive	portatum esse	to have been carried

Again the tense of the participle is in relation to the main verb. The literal sense *having been X-ed* usually sounds awkward in English and is better avoided. Just *X-ed* is often fine:

hostes victi lente discesserunt.
The defeated enemy slowly left.

• This use of *defeated* must of course be distinguished in English from its use as a simple past tense (e.g. *we defeated them*).

Because this participle is passive, it can have an agent and/or instrument like any passive verb (see page 95):

epistulam a senatore missam numquam accepi.
I never received the letter sent by the senator.

The perfect passive participle is often better replaced by a clause beginning *when, after* or *who/which*. Because it refers to something that has already been done when the action described by the main verb happens, it will come out as a *pluperfect* if the main verb is in a past tense. (Compare how a present participle comes out as an imperfect: see page 119.)

milites urbem ab hostibus oppugnatam intraverunt.
The soldiers entered the city which had been attacked by the enemy.

Exercise 52   Perfect passive participle

1 puer de pecunia celata nihil dixit.
2 muri a deis aedificati numquam delebuntur.
3 cives clamoribus territi dormire non poterant.
4 feminam conspectam salutavi.
5 nonne epistulas ab amico tuo missas iam habes?
6 senex servo vocato librum dedit.
7 nautam e nave eiectum tandem servavi.
8 villam ab hostibus incensam vidimus.
9 nolo consumere cibum in illa taberna emptum.
10 verba scripta manent.

COMMON IRREGULAR PERFECT PASSIVE PARTICIPLES

Here are thirty of the most important irregular perfect passive participles, which should be learned (others can be found in the vocabulary, pages 184–98):

participle	*meaning*	*present tense*
actus -a -um*	(having been) done	ago
captus	taken, captured	capio
cognitus	found out	cognosco
coactus	forced	cogo
conspectus	noticed, caught sight of	conspicio
deletus	destroyed	deleo
datus	given	do
ductus	led	duco
factus	made, done	facio
latus	carried	fero
iactus	thrown	iacio
interfectus	killed	interficio
inventus	found	invenio
iussus	ordered	iubeo
lectus	read	lego
missus	sent	mitto
motus	moved	moveo
occisus	killed	occido
oblatus	offered	offero
oppressus	crushed	opprimo
pulsus	driven	pello
positus	placed, put	pono
promissus	promised	promitto
quaesitus	looked for	quaero
raptus	seized	rapio
relictus	left	relinquo
scriptus	written	scribo
versus	turned	verto
visus	seen	video
victus	conquered	vinco

* all are regular 2-1-2 in declension (see page 24)

PERFECT ACTIVE PARTICIPLE (FROM DEPONENT VERBS)

Deponent and semi-deponent verbs (see pages 99–101) have a perfect active participle.

Examples:

deponent

conatus -a -um	having tried	conor
hortatus	having encouraged	hortor
in/e/re-gressus	having gone in/out/back	in/e/re-gredior
progressus	having advanced	progredior
locutus	having spoken	loquor
mortuus	having died	morior
passus	having suffered	patior
profectus	having set out	proficiscor
secutus	having followed	sequor

semi-deponent

gavisus	having rejoiced	gaudeo
solitus	having been accustomed	soleo

Because a perfect active participle is not otherwise available in Latin, this is a useful feature of deponent verbs (see pages 129–31 on ablative absolute).

Again the literal translation *having X-ed* often sounds artificial, and a translation such as *after doing X* or *when they had done X* is often appropriate. (For the way in which a perfect participle comes out like a pluperfect tense when translated as a clause, see page 122.)

• The perfect tense of a deponent verb is like the perfect passive of an ordinary verb (see pages 96 and 99), consisting of the perfect participle with the auxiliary verb *to be*:

rex mortuus est.
The king died (*or* has died).

But it is also possible to read this example as simply an adjective with the present tense of the verb *to be*:

The king is dead.

(Contrast *rex moritur* = the king is dying.)

Exercise 53   Perfect active participle (from deponent verbs)

1   hostes regressi castra sua intraverunt.
2   multas horas locutus senator tandem tacuit.
3   nautae prima hora profecti mox ad portum advenerunt.
4   multa vulnera passus miles mortuus est.
5   milites portas urbis intrare frustra conati abierunt.

FUTURE ACTIVE PARTICIPLE

		about to carry		
		m	*f*	*n*
sg	*nom*	portat-ur-us	portat-ur-a	portat-ur-um
	acc	portat-ur-um	portat-ur-am	portat-ur-um
		etc	*etc*	*etc*
		(regular 2-1-2: see page 24)		

This is *formed from* the perfect passive participle (see pages 121–3), inserting the syllable *-ur-* before the ending, but is *active* in meaning. Similarly for the other conjugations:

2nd	3rd	4th
about to warn	about to drag	about to hear
moniturus -a -um	tracturus -a -um	auditurus -a -um

There is a whole range of possible translations for the future active participle: *about to . . .*, *going to . . .*, *intending to*. There is often a suggestion of purpose. Like other participles, the future active one is often better translated as a clause (for example *when . . .*). Like other participles too, its tense is in relation to that of the main verb, so with a passage set in the past a future participle may come out as (for example) *when they were about to do X*.

The future active participle is similarly used with the imperfect tense of the auxiliary verb *to be* (see page 75) to form a 'made up' finite tense expressing *future in the past*. Using again the analogy of the lift in the multi-storey building, this is going two floors down then looking one up: at some point in the past, something *was going to* happen.

> senex pecuniam celaturus erat.
> The old man was going to hide the money.

• The future participle is used with the infinitive of the verb *to be* to form the future infinitive (see page 134).

• Deponent verbs have a future active participle of normal form, e.g. *conaturus* (= about to try).

Exercise 54 Future active participle

1 morituri te salutamus.
2 nuntius verba imperatoris narraturus omnes tacere iussit.
3 talem cibum numquam dormiturus consumo.
4 milites urbem oppugnaturi signum exspectabant.
5 epistulam difficilem scripturus diu cogitabam.

DISENTANGLING PARTICIPLES

Any kind of participle within a sentence is often better taken out and translated as a subordinate clause, or even made into a separate main clause joined by *and*:

>pater filiae ex urbe discessurae pecuniam dedit.
>The father gave money to his daughter who was about to leave the city.

>milites captivum inventum in castra duxerunt.

lit The soldiers led the (having been) found prisoner into the camp.

but in better English
>The soldiers led the prisoner they had found into the camp.

or When the soldiers had found the prisoner they led him into the camp.

or The soldiers found the prisoner and led him into the camp.

In the second example it is assumed from the context that the prisoner has been found by the soldiers rather than someone else, so the passive participle can be translated by an active verb (see pages 129–30 for this point in relation to ablative absolute).

Exercise 55   Disentangling participles

1 milites urbem tandem captam incenderunt.
2 dominus servum in urbem ductum vendidit.
3 hominem gladio tam graviter vulneratum nemo servare potest.
4 senex uxori cibum offerenti nihil dixit.
5 servus omnia audita senatori nuntiavit.

ABLATIVE ABSOLUTE

This is a phrase consisting of a noun (or pronoun) and participle in the ablative, not linked grammatically with the rest of the sentence. Its name comes from the old sense of *absolute* as *separated* (rather than its modern meaning of *complete*). It is found most commonly with the perfect passive participle, but it can be used with any participle. It describes circumstances that apply when the main action of the sentence happens.

The literal translation *with . . .* is sometimes acceptable:

> naves omnibus civibus spectantibus profectae sunt.
> The ships set out with all the citizens watching.

Sometimes words such as *with* and *having been* can be left out, but the phrase still translated literally:

> his rebus factis, senatores discesserunt.
> These things done, the senators left.

More often it is better (as with other participle phrases) to translate an ablative absolute with a clause. The usual point applies about the tense of the participle being in relation to the tense of the main verb.

> rege locuturo omnes tacuerunt.
> When (*or* Because) the king was about to speak, everyone was silent.

When the ablative absolute contains a perfect passive participle, you need to think carefully about whether to make it into an active verb in English, or leave it passive. Consider two examples:

> his verbis auditis, puellae laetissimae erant.
> *lit*   With these words having been heard the girls were very happy.

Because it is natural to assume from the context that the girls (rather than someone else) had heard the words, it is appropriate to translate:

> When they had heard these words, the girls were very happy.

Contrast this sentence:

> urbe capta cives miserrimi erant.
> *lit*   With the city having been captured the citizens were very miserable.

Here the citizens have obviously not done the capturing (their enemy has), so the translation of the ablative absolute needs to leave it passive:

> Because (*or* When) the city had been captured, the citizens were very miserable.

An ablative absolute commonly comes at the beginning of a sentence. It may be separated off by a comma. It often incorporates a connecting relative (see page 116).

> quo audito, omnes senatorem laudaverunt.
>
> *lit*   With which (thing) having been heard, they all praised the senator.
>
> *i.e.*   When they had heard this, they all praised the senator.

The verb *to be* does not have a present participle, so ablative absolute phrases are sometimes found in which *being* needs to be supplied as the literal translation (and no actual participle is in the sentence):

> Caesare duce hostes vicimus.
>
> *lit*   With Caesar being leader we conquered the enemy.
>
> *or in better English*
>
> With Caesar as leader . . . *or* Under Caesar's leadership . . .

• If a noun referring to a person is in the ablative without a preposition, it is very likely to be part of an ablative absolute.

• A participle phrase is only put in the ablative absolute if it cannot go into any other case which would relate it to the rest of the sentence. Sometimes a phrase that looks like an ablative absolute is actually dative:

> puellis auxilium petentibus cibum dedi.
> I gave food to the girls who were seeking help.

• Conversely, a participle phrase may be ablative (for example because it follows a preposition), but not ablative absolute:

> nihil scio de femina lacrimanti.
> I know nothing about the woman who is weeping.

Note here that the participle has the ablative singular ending *-i* rather than *-e* because it is being used purely as an adjective (see pages 25 and 118), whereas in an ablative absolute the participle is doing a job like that of a verb in a clause, and has the ablative ending *-e*.

• The fact that ablative absolutes are commonly translated by clauses beginning *who* . . ., *when* . . ., *because* . . . etc illustrates how Latin can express the same meaning in different ways. So for example *his verbis dictis* followed by a third person singular verb means the same as *cum haec verba dixisset* (= when he/she had said these words): see page 152.

Exercise 56   Ablative absolute

1 his verbis dictis, nuntius discessit.
2 regina horto deleto tristissima erat.
3 militibus paratis imperator proficisci constituit.
4 servis venditis cenam ipse paro.
5 consule adveniente, cives gaudebant.
6 puella laetior erat epistula lecta.
7 hostibus visis omnes timebamus.
8 cives clamoribus auditis auxilium statim miserunt.
9 imperatore morituro novum ducem legere debemus.
10 pueris tacere iussis senex villam intravit.

INDIRECT STATEMENT

A statement is an ordinary sentence that is not a question or command. A *direct* statement may be the actual quoted words of a speaker:

The messenger said 'The Romans have captured the city'.

Or it may be simply something the narrator tells us:

After a long siege the Romans captured the city.

An *indirect* statement *reports* someone's words or thoughts (hence it is also called a *reported* statement):

The messenger said that the Romans had captured the city.

This historian claims that after a long siege the Romans captured the city.

English inserts the word *that* (though it can be omitted), then in effect starts a new sentence with its own subject and verb. Latin does it in a different way: the subject of the indirect statement becomes *accusative*, and the verb becomes *infinitive*. Hence this construction is commonly referred to as *accusative and infinitive*.

An accusative and infinitive is possible in English with some verbs:

I believe the story to be true.

This sentence reports my original thought *The story is true*.

The judge declared the winner to be this girl.

This sentence reports his original statement *The winner is this girl*. It may seem strange that a subject should be accusative, but imagine these sentences cut short: in *I believe the story* or *The judge declared the winner* it should be obvious that *story* and *winner* cannot be nominative.

• In these examples *I* and *judge* are nominative: a sentence can only introduce a *second* nominative (after the main subject) if it has a second *finite* verb, with a person ending (see pages 2 and 68–9): the *infinitive* as its name implies is not finite.

In English the accusative and infinitive is not found very often, but in Latin it is used for *all* indirect statements. It is one of the most common of all constructions, and failure to recognise it is one of the main sources of confusion and error in GCSE.

Because this construction is used to report original direct statements that might have verbs in any tense, Latin needs to use a range of infinitives. See page 74 for the present active infinitive:

1st	portare	to carry
2nd	monere	to warn
3rd	trahere	to drag
4th	audire	to hear

See page 98 for the present passive infinitive:

1st	portari	to be carried
2nd	moneri	to be warned
3rd	trahi	to be dragged
4th	audiri	to be heard

These present infinitives are common in various contexts. Other infinitives are found mainly in indirect statements.

More infinitives

The *perfect active infinitive* (literally *to have X-ed*) is formed from the *perfect stem* (see page 78) plus *-isse*:

1st	portavisse	to have carried
2nd	monuisse	to have warned
3rd	traxisse	to have dragged
4th	audivisse	to have heard

The *perfect passive infinitive* (literally *to have been X-ed*) is formed from the *perfect passive participle* (see page 121) with the infinitive of the verb *to be* (see page 76):

1st	portatum* esse	to have been carried
2nd	monitum* esse	to have been warned
3rd	tractum* esse	to have been dragged
4th	auditum* esse	to have been heard

The future active infinitive (literally *to be going to* X) is formed from the future active participle (see page 126), again with the infinitive of the verb *to be* (see page 76):

1st	portaturum* esse	to be going to carry
2nd	moniturum* esse	to be going to warn
3rd	tracturum* esse	to be going to drag
4th	auditurum* esse	to be going to hear

*The participle is naturally accusative in indirect statement, but can be any gender, singular or plural (according to normal 2-1-2 endings: see page 24), agreeing with the subject of the infinitive. In the accusative and infinitive construction, the possibilities are as follows (using the perfect passive infinitive of *porto* as an example, but the pattern of endings applies to all perfect passive and future active infinitives):

	m	*f*	*n*
sg	portatum esse	portatam esse	portatum esse
pl	portatos esse	portatas esse	portata esse

Indirect statements are most obviously introduced by verbs meaning *say*, *announce*, etc. But this construction is used also with verbs such as *think* and *know* – any verb that expresses the use of words, intellect, or the senses (the statement reported need not actually have been spoken). Look out for it after the following:

dico	I say
narro	I tell
nuntio	I announce
respondeo	I reply
promitto	I promise
audio	I hear
video	I see
cognosco	I find out
intellego	I understand
scio	I know
credo*	I believe
sentio	I feel

*In this construction, *credo* like other verbs is followed by the accusative and infinitive (overriding the usual rule that it takes a dative).

The tense of the infinitive is that of the original direct statement (the words of a speaker, or the implied statement representing someone's thoughts). To translate correctly you need to go through a two-stage process: thinking what the Latin says literally, then how this comes out in English.

If the introductory verb (the verb of *saying* etc, which is the main verb of the sentence, and can come anywhere within it) is present tense, this is straightforward:

>   nuntius dicit navem appropinquare.
> *lit*   The messenger says the ship to be approaching.
> *i.e.*   The messenger says that the ship is approaching.

>   audio hostes fugisse.
> *lit*   I hear the enemy to have fled.
> *i.e.*   I hear that the enemy have fled.

>   credo has ancillas bene laboraturas esse.
> *lit*   I believe these slave-girls to be going to work well.
> *i.e.*   I believe that these slave-girls will work well.

Exercise 57   Indirect statement (with present tense main verb)

1   nuntius dicit homines crudeles ibi habitare.
2   video magnam turbam in forum convenire.
3   hic miles nuntiat urbem hostium captam esse.
4   audio omnes eos servos a domino custodiri.
5   nonne credis milites nostros fortiter pugnaturos esse?

If the introductory verb is past tense (as it much more commonly is), the infinitive still has the tense of what was originally said or thought, but an adjustment has to be made in translation. This happens in English too: the direct statement *The ship is approaching* is reported afterwards as *The messenger said that the ship was approaching*. So if the introductory verb is in any past tense, the infinitive *moves a tense back* in translation:

>   a present infinitive is translated as an imperfect tense
>   a perfect infinitive is translated as a pluperfect tense
>   a future infinitive is translated as a 'future in the past' (*was/were going to*)

Again the secret is to think first what the Latin says literally, then recast this as natural English.

>   nuntius dixit navem appropinquare.
> *lit*   The messenger said the ship to be approaching.
> *i.e.*   The messenger said that the ship *was* approaching.

audivi hostes fugisse.
lit   I heard the enemy to have fled.
i.e.   I heard that the enemy *had* fled.

credebam has ancillas bene laboraturas esse.
lit   I believed these slave-girls to be going to work well.
i.e.   I believed that these slave-girls *were going to* (or *would*) work well.

The accusative subject must always be there in this construction, and indeed is one way of recognising it. If the subject of the infinitive is the same as the subject of the introductory verb, a reflexive pronoun is used, usually *se* (see page 42):

nuntius dixit se quam celerrime cucurrisse.
The messenger said that he had run as quickly as possible.

If *he* had referred to someone else, i.e. had not been reflexive, *eum* (see page 43) would have been used instead:

femina, quae servum amabat, dixit eum bene laboravisse.
The woman, who liked the slave, said that he had worked well.

Because the infinitive has an accusative subject and may also have a direct object, two different accusatives may come one after the other. In such a sentence the first accusative will be the subject, the second one the object:

credo senem pueros laudavisse.
I believe that the old man praised the boys.

• Indirect statement can continue with another infinitive after a semi-colon (representing an original direct statement consisting of more than a single sentence):

nuntius dixit bellum confectum esse; hostes fugisse; se haec a rege ipso audivisse.
The messenger said that the war was finished, that the enemy had fled, and that he had heard these things from the king himself.

• A passive version of the indirect statement can be used. In this case the subject is nominative:

servus dicitur stultus esse.
The slave is said to be stupid.

If a perfect passive or future active infinitive is used like this, the participle forming part of it will be nominative:

epistula dicitur missa esse.
The letter is said to have been sent.

• Deponent and semi-deponent verbs (see pages 99–101) have a perfect active infinitive with the form of a perfect passive one, and a future active infinitive of the normal type.

credo neminem me secutum esse.
I believe that no-one followed me.

Exercise 58   Indirect statement (with past tense main verb)

1   miles nuntiavit hostes fugere.
2   cives audiverunt hostes fugisse.
3   puer dixit fratrem suum tandem dormire.
4   patrem meum fortissimum esse intellexi.
5   puella dixit se donum tuum amare.
6   mercator dixit se multam pecuniam in via amisisse.
7   scivistine illam domum venditam esse?
8   rex nesciebat omnes amicos fugisse.
9   senator dixit servum multos cives necavisse.
10   heri credidi nos in magno periculo futuros esse.

Exercise 59   Indirect statement (assorted tenses)

1   amicos discessuros esse forte cognovimus.
2   puellasne omnes adesse vides?
3   rex promisit se auxilium nobis missurum esse.
4   audio muros deletos esse.
5   femina dixit se sine marito iter fecisse.
6   spero patrem pecuniam mihi missurum esse.
7   nuntius narravit milites nostros multa mala passos esse.
8   neminem appropinquare sensi.
9   novum templum aedificari video.
10   senex dixit se nihil audivisse; uxorem perterritam fuisse; domum incensam esse.

IMPERFECT SUBJUNCTIVE

The term *subjunctive* is not very informative: it means *joined under* (i.e. *bolted on*, as an alternative form of the verb), but this gives no clue about its use. It is basically a form of the verb that expresses a *possibility* rather than a fact (something that *might* happen, or *might* be the reason for something else).

The normal form in contrast is called *indicative* because it does state or *indicate* a fact (all ordinary verb forms with a tense and a person ending are indicative, though they are usually only described as such when they are being contrasted with the subjunctive).

The translation of the imperfect subjunctive varies according to the construction it is in.

It is very easy to form and recognise. The basic person endings (*-m, -s, -t, -mus, -tis, -nt*: see page 69) are stuck onto the infinitive.

sg	*1*	portare-m	monere-m	trahere-m	audire-m
	2	portare-s	monere-s	trahere-s	audire-s
	3	portare-t	*etc*	*etc*	*etc*
pl	*1*	portare-mus			
	2	portare-tis			
	3	portare-nt			

This also works for irregular verbs (see pages 76 and 85–8):

infinitive	*imperfect subjunctive*
esse	essem -es -et *etc*
posse	possem
ire	irem
velle	vellem
nolle	nollem
malle	mallem
ferre	ferrem

The passive form of the imperfect subjunctive is made by changing the active endings to passive ones in the usual way (see page 91):

sg	*1*	portare-r	monere-r	trahere-r	audire-r
	2	portare-ris	monere-ris	trahere-ris	audire-ris
	3	portare-tur	*etc*	*etc*	*etc*
pl	*1*	portare-mur			
	2	portare-mini			
	3	portare-ntur			

PURPOSE CLAUSES

One of the most common uses of the imperfect subjunctive is in a purpose clause, explaining the aim with which something was done.

I went to Rome to see the emperor.

He worked hard in order to get an A*.

Latin does not use the infinitive for this as you might expect from English, but instead uses the word *ut* (= in order to) with the imperfect subjunctive.

Translation as an infinitive in English often works if the subject of the purpose clause is the same as the subject of the main verb of the sentence:

senex ad urbem ambulavit ut librum emeret.
lit   The old man walked to the city in order that he might buy a book.
i.e.   The old man walked to the city to buy a book.

If the purpose clause has a new subject, a translation such as *in order that* or *so that* is needed, putting *might*, *would* or *could* (expressing a *possibility*) with the verb:

femina totum diem laborabat ut liberi cibum haberent.
The woman was working all day so that her children would have food.

A negative purpose clause uses *ne* (= in order not to) instead of *ut*:

noctem exspectavimus ne ab hostibus videremur.
We waited for night in order not to be seen by the enemy.

• A purpose clause is sometimes called a *final* clause, not because it comes last thing in the sentence (though it often does) but because it tells us the *end* in view, in the old sense of *aim*.

• A purpose clause needs to be carefully distinguished from a result clause (also using *ut* and the imperfect subjunctive) which stresses the outcome rather than the intention: see page 147.

• The construction for a purpose clause is the same as for an indirect command (see pages 144–5), and a negative purpose clause is also the same as the construction with a verb of fearing (see page 149).

• Note that *ut* with an ordinary indicative verb (or no verb at all) means *as*.

• For other ways of expressing purpose see pages 142–3.

Exercise 60   Purpose clauses

1   pueri in via manere volebant ut puellas spectarent.
2   Romam ire constitui ut fratrem meum viderem.
3   femina clamavit ut ab omnibus audiretur.
4   servi diu laborabant ut novos muros aedificarent.
5   in taberna manebam ne verba imperatoris audirem.
6   rex illos custodes habuit ne ab hostibus necaretur.
7   amici fideles advenerunt ut nos servarent.
8   senex pecuniam in terra celavit ne uxor inveniret.
9   hi mortui sunt ut nos viveremus.
10 vos docebamini ut alios doceretis.

OTHER WAYS OF EXPRESSING PURPOSE

(1) *ad* with the gerundive

This is another way of expressing purpose: a less common alternative to an *ut* clause (see page 140). A *gerundive* is an adjective made from a verb (not counted as a participle, but with similar characteristics). Its literal meaning is *needing to be X-ed*: it is *passive* and has the idea of *necessity*. It does not have a tense, but refers to a sort of possible future (just as an imperative does: see page 102) – something that has not happened yet, but should. It is formed from the verb stem, the characteristic vowel(s) for the conjugation (see page 71) and *-ndus* (with normal 2-1-2 endings: see page 24). Thus:

portandus -a -um	needing to be carried
monendus -a -um	needing to be warned
trahendus -a -um	needing to be dragged
audiendus -a -um	needing to be heard

It is easy to recognise because few other Latin words have the combination of letters *-nd-* with vowels either side. The gerundive has various jobs in more advanced Latin, but the only use of it met at GCSE is with *ad* to express purpose. This use of *ad* for an aim or purpose is an extension of its normal idea of *motion towards*.

> misit nuntios ad regem necandum.
> *lit*   He sent messengers (with a view) to the king needing to be killed.
> *i.e.*   He sent messengers to kill the king.

• This sentence means the same as *misit nuntios ut regem necarent*.

The English translation of the gerundive used after *ad* should get away both from the passive and from the idea of necessity. This may seem a complex change, but if you think of the basic sense of each word (*ad* = to, *necare* = kill, *rex* = king), taking the noun as the object of the verb expressed by the gerundive, the meaning should be obvious.

Further examples:

> domum festinavi ad pecuniam quaerendam.
> I hurried home to look for the money.

> senex filiam misit ad canem inveniendum.
> The old man sent his daughter to find the dog.

visne ad villam meam venire ad vinum bibendum?
Do you want to come to my house to drink wine?

• Note in each of these sentences how the gerundive *agrees* (see page 27) with the accusative noun.

Exercise 61   *Ad* with the gerundive to express purpose

1   senex ad tabernam ambulabat ad cibum emendum.
2   nuntius venerat ad verba regis narranda.
3   leo lente progrediebatur ad hominem consumendum.
4   puer in via stabat ad puellam salutandam.
5   consul surrexit ad cives de periculo monendos.

---

(2) *dum* with the imperfect subjunctive

In an ordinary time clause (see page 111) *dum* means *while*, and is used with a present tense verb to express the idea of one thing going on when another happens. But *dum* can also (less commonly) be used with an imperfect subjunctive to mean *until*, implying purpose as well as time:

> cives in foro manebant dum senator adveniret.
> The citizens waited in the forum until the senator arrived (*or* could arrive).
> *or*   The citizens waited in the forum for the senator to arrive.

This is in effect a disguised purpose clause: they waited *so that he could* arrive with them still there (he may or may not actually have done so); as usual, the subjunctive here emphasises a possibility rather than a fact.

Exercise 62   *Dum* with the imperfect subjunctive to express time/purpose

1   hunc librum legebam dum omnia verba intellegerem.
2   Romae manebamus dum imperatorem videremus.
3   dux noster exspectabat dum omnes naves convenirent.
4   captivos in castris tenuimus dum totam rem narrarent.
5   puellam domi manere iussi dum epistulam meam acciperet.

INDIRECT COMMANDS

For direct commands using the imperative see page 102. An *indirect* command reports a command, usually one previously given (compare page 132 on indirect statements, and page 154 on indirect questions).

| *direct:* | Be quiet! |
| *indirect:* | I told the children to be quiet. |

The verb *iubeo* (= I order) uses the infinitive for an indirect command just as English does:

> senator cives audire iussit.
> The senator ordered to citizens to listen.

Most other verbs use a clause with *ut* and the imperfect subjunctive, just like a purpose clause (see page 140). Note that *impero* (also = I order) takes a dative, because the idea is of giving an order *to* someone:

> senator civibus imperavit ut audirent.
> The senator ordered the citizens to listen.

• The construction is the same as for a purpose clause, because the underlying thought is the same. There is almost a pun on the word *order* in English: the senator gave an *order* to the citizens in *order* that they might listen, i.e. to achieve that purpose. Sometimes it is hard to tell the difference:

> epistulam amico scripsi ut in montes effugeret.

This could be read as a purpose clause:

> I wrote a letter to my friend <u>so that he could</u> escape into the mountains

Or as an indirect command:

> I wrote a letter to my friend <u>telling him to</u> escape into the mountains.

Nonetheless the two constructions are in practice classed separately.

A *command* in the grammatical sense can be a polite request or suggestion, rather than an actual order. Thus indirect commands can be introduced by a wide range of verbs, for example:

| hortor | I encourage, I urge |
| moneo | I warn, I advise |

oro   I beg
persuadeo   I persuade (+ *dat*)
rogo   I ask

A negative indirect command uses *ne* instead of *ut*, just as a negative purpose clause does:

feminas monui ne in foro manerent.
I advised the women not to stay in the forum.

Exercise 63   Indirect commands

1 senator nautas in portu laborare iussit.
2 dominus servo imperavit ut cibum in hortum portaret.
3 senex pueros ne trans viam ambularent monuit.
4 ancilla a patre meo iussa est cenam optimam parare.
5 civibus persuadere volui ne talia verba audirent.
6 imperator militibus imperavit ut per terram hostium lente progrederentur.
7 a principe rogatus eram ut in villa eius paucos dies manerem.
8 dux milites hortabatur ut ferocius pugnarent.
9 nonne a domino saepe monebaris ne in templo curreres?
10 rex omnes fugientes revocari iussit.

Exercise 64   Purpose clauses and indirect commands (revision)

1 matrem rogavi ut pecuniam mihi daret.
2 dux milites misit ut castra hostium invenirent.
3 multos dies in castris manebamus ne ab hostibus videremur.
4 his servis imperavi ut laborem celeriter conficerent.
5 senex nos monebat ne prope flumen villam aedificaremus.
6 prima luce profecti sumus ut ante noctem adveniremus.
7 senator cives hortabatur ut verbis suis crederent.
8 puer in montes fugit ne a patre inveniretur.
9 haec verba vobis locutus sum ut totam rem intellegeretis.
10 puellae ut de his rebus scriberet persuadere conatus sum.

RESULT CLAUSES

A result clause focuses on the outcome of an action:

He ran so fast that he won the prize.

It is recognised by a signpost word (*so* etc) in the first half of the sentence, then *ut* for *that* introducing the second half (the actual result clause), with the verb in the imperfect subjunctive to describe a result in the past.

The most common signpost words are:

tam	so	(*with an adjective or adverb*)
adeo	so much, to such an extent	(*with a verb*)
ita	in such a way	(*with a verb*)

haec puella tam fortis erat ut omnes eam laudarent.
This girl was so brave that everyone praised her.

puer adeo clamabat ut ab omnibus audiretur.
The boy was shouting so much that he was heard by everyone.

senator ita loquebatur ut praemia acciperet.
The senator used to speak in such a way that he received prizes.

Note also some more specialised signpost words:

tantus	so big	(*used instead of* tam magnus)
tot	so many	(*used instead of* tam multi)
talis	such, of such a sort	

• Of these, *tantus* is normal 2-1-2 in declension (see page 24) and *talis* is a third declension adjective like *fortis* (see page 25); *tot* is indeclinable.

• Note the distinction between *tot* and the plural of *tantus*:

tot equi	so many horses
tanti equi	such big horses

• Note the similarity of these signpost words beginning *t-* to the question words beginning *qu-* (see page 105), which they can also be used to answer:

question		*answer*	
quantus	how big?	tantus	so big
quot	how many?	tot	so many
qualis	what sort?	talis	of such a sort, this sort

• Because a result clause depends so importantly on the signpost word in the first half, it is sometimes also called a *consecutive* (= following on) clause.

A result clause must be carefully distinguished from a purpose clause (which also uses *ut* and the subjunctive: see page 140). It has a different emphasis:

(1) *purpose clause:*

The boy worked hard in order to get an A*.

That was the aim, but might not be the result: he could have been unlucky, or not worked quite hard enough.

(2) *result clause:*

The boy worked so hard that he got an A*.

That was the result, but might not have been the aim: he could have been unduly modest and aiming only for a B.

A purpose clause and a result clause both normally use *ut* and (in the examples you will meet in GCSE) the imperfect subjunctive. But if the clause contains a negative, there is an important difference: a negative purpose clause uses *ne* instead of *ut*, but a negative result clause uses *non* as well as *ut* (this is the only place where *ut* and *non* are used together).

cibus talis erat ut eum edere non possem.
The food was such (*or* so bad) that I could not eat it.

Note here that flexibility is needed in translation of *talis* according to context.

• On the use of negatives in general see page 157–8, and on the different uses of *ut* see page 163.

Exercise 65   Result clauses

1   dominus tam saevus erat ut omnes servi timerent.
2   ancilla tam bene laborabat ut ab omnibus laudaretur.
3   tanta erat turba ut progredi non possemus.
4   adeo timebamus ut nihil faceremus.
5   equus talis erat ut nemo tenere posset.
6   nuntius tam celeriter locutus est ut verba eius iterum audire cogeremur.
7   tot epistulas acceperam ut non possem omnibus respondere.
8   miles adeo vulneratus erat ut mox moreretur.
9   tanti erant custodes ut nemo portam intrare vellet.
10 puer tam stultus erat ut nihil intellegeret.

VERBS OF FEARING

The verb *timeo* (= I fear) can take a direct object or an infinitive, as in English:

omnes nautae periculum maris timebant.
All the sailors feared the danger of the sea.

cur templum intrare times?
Why are you afraid to enter the temple?

But it also commonly takes a clause using *ne* and the imperfect subjunctive, expressing what someone feared might happen. In form this construction is like a negative purpose clause (or indirect command) but is not negative in English. The old-fashioned word *lest* gives the sense exactly, but because it is no longer in common use is better avoided: modern English just says *that*.

diu timebamus ne urbs nostra caperetur.
We feared for a long time that our city would be captured.

• The reason a negative was used in the first place (though not translated as such) is that fearing is thought of as *hoping that something would not* happen.

• Note that *timeo* means *I fear*; *terreo* means *I frighten (someone)*. The English *I am frightened* (describing a state of mind) would normally be represented in Latin by *timeo*. Note however that *perterritus* (the perfect passive participle of the compound *perterreo*, literally *I frighten thoroughly*) is used as an adjective meaning *terrified*.

It is also possible (though much less common) to express a negative fear, that something might *not* happen (i.e. you *hoped it would* happen). For this Latin uses *ne* followed by *non*: the only place where *ne* and *non* are found together.

timebam ne custos clamores non audiret.
I feared that the guard might not hear the shouts.

Exercise 66   Verbs of fearing

1   timebam ne hostes advenirent.
2   timui e castris egredi.
3   puer ne inveniretur timebat.
4   timebamus ne imperator nos videret.
5   timuistine ne praemium non acciperes?

PLUPERFECT SUBJUNCTIVE

This is the second most common tense of the subjunctive after the imperfect, and the only other one needed for GCSE. The *imperfect* subjunctive is formed by adding the basic person endings (see page 69) to the *present* infinitive (see pages 74 and 138). By a similar process the *pluperfect* subjunctive is formed by adding the same basic person endings to the *perfect* infinitive (see page 133), again producing a tense one back from the infinitive involved.

The imperfect subjunctive cannot be translated in isolation because it depends on its job in a construction. The pluperfect subjunctive on the other hand translates just like a normal pluperfect. Expect to see it in two constructions described below: *cum* clauses (page 152) and indirect questions (pages 154–5).

sg	*1*	portavisse-m	monuisse-m	traxisse-m	audivisse-m
	2	portavisse-s	monuisse-s	traxisse-s	audivisse-s
	3	portavisse-t	*etc*	*etc*	*etc*
pl	*1*	portavisse-mus			
	2	portavisse-tis			
	3	portavisse-nt			

Again this works also for irregular verbs (see pages 76 and 85–8), for example:

verb	*perfect tense*	*perfect infinitive*	*pluperfect subjunctive*
sum	fui	fuisse	fuissem
possum	potui	potuisse	potuissem
eo	i(v)i	iisse	i(v)issem
volo	volui	voluisse	voluissem
nolo	nolui	noluisse	noluissem
malo	malui	maluisse	maluissem
fero	tuli	tulisse	tulissem

The passive form of the pluperfect subjunctive simply takes the ordinary pluperfect passive (see pages 96–7) and puts the auxiliary verb, which is the imperfect of *to be*, into its subjunctive form (see page 138):

sg	1	portatus essem
	2	portatus esses
	3	portatus esset
pl	1	portati essemus
	2	portati essetis
	3	portati essent

Similarly for the other conjugations:

2nd	monitus essem
3rd	tractus essem
4th	auditus essem

As with the ordinary pluperfect passive (see pages 96–7), the perfect passive participle (see page 121) forming the first part of this tense agrees in number and gender with the subject of the sentence.

CUM CLAUSES

Clauses telling us *when* or *why* something happened commonly have a word such as *ubi* (= when) or *quod* (= because) with an ordinary indicative verb (see pages 111 and 113).

> ubi Romam adveni, de morte imperatoris audivi.
> When I (had) arrived in Rome, I heard about the death of the emperor.

> servus, quod dormiebat, nihil audivit.
> The slave, because he was asleep, heard nothing.

The first example states that two things happened one after the other. The second tells us one thing that is definitely the reason for the other. Indicative verbs (see page 138) are appropriate because facts are being stated.

In either of these sentences *cum* (translated *when* or *since*) with the appropriate tense of the subjunctive could have been used instead:

> cum Romam advenissem, de morte imperatoris audivi.

> servus, cum dormiret, nihil audivit.

In practice the meaning would be virtually the same as in the previous versions. The slight difference of emphasis is to convey a *suggested reason*: it was *only* by arriving then that I heard the news (and so not just a coincidence of time); it was *presumably* because the slave was asleep (rather than that he was stone deaf or very drunk) that he heard nothing.

• Note in the first example that *ubi* is used with a perfect tense indicative verb (though this can be translated like a pluperfect: see page 111), but the *cum* version uses the pluperfect subjunctive (because the thought here *is* 'in a situation when X had happened, Y happened', rather than 'after X happened, Y happened').

Cum clauses are very common. The imperfect or pluperfect subjunctive translates according to sense, coming out as the same tense in English. The word *since* is favoured because it suggests 'a *when* that is also a *because*'. (This use of *since* in English must be distinguished from its other sense *from the time when*.)

• Note that this *cum* is a completely separate word from the preposition *cum* used with the ablative and meaning *with* (see pages 62 and 162): these are *homonyms*.

Exercise 67 *Cum* clauses

1 cives, cum hostes urbi appropinquarent, perterriti erant.
2 senex, cum ad forum ambularet, multam pecuniam invenit.
3 illis hominibus non credidi cum stulti essent.
4 laeti eramus cum novum consilium intellexissemus.
5 cum omnes feminae advenissent, a viris salutatae sunt.
6 rex, cum iam discedere constituisset, hoc statim fecit.
7 cum montem ascenderem vulnus grave accepi.
8 dominus, cum totam rem audivisset, servum fidelem laudavit.
9 liberi gaudebant cum nihil scribere deberent.
10 nonne iratus eras cum murum deletum conspexisses?

INDIRECT QUESTIONS

This construction reports a direct question (see pages 104–6) previously asked, just as an indirect statement reports a statement (see pages 132–7) and an indirect command reports a command (see pages 144–5):

direct:	Why are you silent?
indirect:	I asked the slave why he was silent.

Here Latin moves a tense back in changing from the direct to the reported form, just like English does (contrast indirect statement, where the infinitive retains the tense of the original direct statement). The verb in the indirect question is imperfect or pluperfect subjunctive: a present tense in the direct question comes out as an imperfect, a past tense as a pluperfect. Each translates naturally into English.

direct:	cur taces?
	Why are you silent?
indirect:	servum rogavi cur taceret.
	I asked the slave why he was silent.
direct:	quis epistulam scripsit?
	Who wrote the letter?
indirect:	senex filiam rogavit quis epistulam scripsisset.
	The old man asked his daughter who had written the letter.

The question words asking for specific information (e.g. *why, who, what, where, how*: see page 105) are used in indirect questions just as in direct ones.

With questions asking if something is the case (to which the answer will be *Yes* or *No*), there is a very important difference. *Direct* questions (see page 104) can be slanted according to the answer the questioner hopes for:

-ne (*added to first word*)	is it the case?	(*open*)
nonne	surely . . . ?	(*hoping for the answer* Yes)
num	surely . . . not?	(*hoping for the answer* No)

In an *indirect* question this distinction cannot be shown, and <u>any</u> question to which the answer will be *Yes* or *No* is (rather confusingly) introduced by *num*, here meaning *whether*. Note therefore the important rule (see also page 162):

| num | *in a <u>direct</u> question* | surely not? |
| | *in an <u>indirect</u> question* | whether |

senem rogavi num fratrem meum vidisset.
I asked the old man whether he had seen my brother.

The original direct question reported here might have been a *-ne, nonne,* or *num* type: all come out the same in the indirect form.

• Note that *if* is another possible translation of *num* in an indirect question, but it should not be confused with *si* (= if) which is used only in a conditional clause (see page 114).

An indirect question is often used when the original direct question is only implied:

difficile erat nobis cognoscere quid accidisset.
It was difficult for us to find out what had happened.

Here the direct question *What happened?* might have existed only in our minds. A verb suggesting *asking* need not be involved at all:

puer nuntiavit quid fecisset.
The boy reported what he had done.

Here the idea is that he said *what it was* that he had done, again answering an implied question *What did you do?* An indirect question can be harder to spot than some constructions, but in practice this does not matter because it usually translates naturally into English.

• Note the difference between an indirect question and a relative clause (see pages 54–6):

(1) *indirect question*
    puellam rogavi quem ibi vidisset.
    I asked the girl whom she had seen there.

(2) *relative clause*
    puella nihil dicere poterat de homine quem ibi viderat.
    The girl could say nothing about the man whom she had seen there.

Exercise 68   Indirect questions

1   pueros rogavi num senem servare conati essent.
2   nemo scivit quid agerem.
3   paterne cognovit ubi heri esses?
4   mater me iterum quid facerem rogavit.
5   imperator cognoscere voluit quis naves hostium vidisset.
6   intellegere non poteram quid ibi faceretur.
7   dominus nesciebat quomodo omnes servi fugissent.
8   filium meum rogavi num abire vellet.
9   cives tandem audiverunt quid a rege dictum esset.
10   servum rogavi num vinum bibisset.

NEGATIVES

The normal negative is *non* and its normal position is just in front of the verb:

>   aquam non amo.
>   I do not like water.

If *non* is put elsewhere in the sentence, it negatives the word it is just in front of:

>   non aquam sed vinum amo.
>   I like not water but wine.

Note the paired negatives *nec . . . nec* (or *neque . . . neque*) = neither . . . nor:

>   nec aquam nec vinum amo.
>   I like neither water nor wine.
>   *or* I do not like either water or wine.

The negative for a possibility rather than a fact is *ne*. This is used (instead of *ut*) for a negative purpose clause (see page 140):

>   servus e villa cucurrit ne a domino videretur.
>   The slave ran out of the house in order not to be seen by his master.

Exactly the same construction is used for a negative indirect command (see page 145):

>   senex pueris imperavit ne in templo clamarent.
>   The old man ordered the boys not to shout in the temple.

Other subjunctive constructions, i.e. result clause (page 147), *cum* clause (page 152), and indirect question (pages 154–5), use the normal negative *non*.

No as the opposite of *Yes* is *minime* (adverb of *minimus*, also used in its literal sense *very little, least*). *No* as an adjective meaning *not any* is *nullus*. For the pronouns *nemo* (= no-one) and *nihil* (= nothing), see page 60.

• Note that *numquam* (= never) is the negative of *umquam* (= ever).

• Note the plural adjective *nonnulli -ae -a* = some, several (literally a double negative *not no*).

• Note that *ne* is also used after a verb of fearing, but is not translated as a negative: see page 149.

• For negative direct commands using *noli* (plural *nolite*) see page 102.

• For the direct question words *nonne* (= surely?) and *num* (= surely not?) see page 104.

Exercise 69   Negatives

1   Romani talia non faciunt.
2   captivus celeriter fugit ne iterum caperetur.
3   non omnes haec intellegunt.
4   puellam rogavi cur senatori non respondisset.
5   servis imperavi ne hunc cibum consumerent.

TRANSLATING COMPLEX SENTENCES

Latin tends not to tell a story in a series of short sentences (or clauses equivalent to separate sentences, joined by *and* or *but*), preferring instead more complex sentences with one *main* clause (that could stand alone) and one or more *subordinate* clauses (that would not make sense in isolation). Here are some typical examples of subordinate clauses:

(1)   When we had arrived in Rome . . .
(2)   . . . to find the book
(3)   If you give me the money . . .
(4)   . . . in order to guard the walls
(5)   . . . whom I saw yesterday
(6)   Although I had heard nothing . . .
(7)   . . . that she understood everything
(8)   . . . who had sent the letter

Try identifying which type of clause each one is (some could be more than one). Many of the constructions described in this book count as subordinate clauses.

To find your way through a difficult sentence, try to find the main clause; bracket off (mentally or on paper) the subordinate bit or bits, then decide how to put the whole thing together. Thought needs to be given to appropriate expression in English.

> Romani, postquam in castra advenerunt, cibum quaesiverunt.
> *lit*   The Romans, after they arrived in the camp, looked for food.

A very common mistake in GCSE is to write:

> The Romans, after they arrived in the camp, they looked for food.

This is wrong because it puts in too many subjects (*The Romans . . . they . . . they*). There are two verbs, and two clauses, so there can only be two subjects. But the candidate who made this mistake sensed rightly that the literal translation sounds awkward. The best solution here is to put *the Romans* inside the subordinate clause:

> After the Romans arrived in the camp, they looked for food.

A participle often needs to be translated as subordinate clause: see pages 119, 122 and 126. A perfect passive participle can be translated as an active verb if it is clear from the context that the action has been done by the person who is subject of the sentence:

> puer puellam conspectam salutavit.
> *lit*   The boy greeted the having been caught sight of girl.
> *i.e.* The boy greeted the girl he had caught sight of.

An ablative absolute (see pages 129–31) is often translated as a subordinate clause:

> his verbis dictis nuntius discessit.
> When he had said these words the messenger left.

But it is also acceptable to make two main clauses, joined by *and*: the clauses are now *co-ordinated* (i.e. both of equal importance):

> The messenger said these words and left.

Double subordination is when one subordinate clause has another clause (or an ablative absolute, or other participle phrase) inside it. It is usually better in English to make the two subordinate elements parallel to one another:

> milites misi ut rege interfecto urbem caperent.
> *lit*   I sent soldiers in order that, with the king having been killed, they could capture the city.
> *i.e.* I sent soldiers to kill the king and capture the city.

Here the ablative absolute has been treated like another purpose clause.

> cum senator epistula lecta surrexisset, omnes tacuerunt.
> *lit*   When the senator, with the letter having been read, had stood up, everyone was silent.
> *i.e.* When the senator had read the letter and stood up, everyone was silent.

Here the ablative absolute has been treated like another *cum* clause.

> deus dixit hunc hominem, Romam ingressum, regem futurum esse.
> *lit*   The god said that this man, having entered Rome, would be king.
> *i.e.* The god said that this man would enter Rome and be king.

Here the participle phrase has been treated like another indirect statement. Sometimes a double subordination can be retained in English:

> cum omnes qui audire volebant advenissent, senator loqui coepit.

When everyone who wanted to listen had arrived, the senator began to speak.

Here the relative clause has been translated literally, inside the *cum* clause.

Exercise 70   Complex sentences

1   haec puella promittit se labore confecto ceteras docturam esse.
2   Romani, cum bellum eo loco gererent, montem ascenderunt ut castra hostium subito oppugnarent.
3   verbis nuntii auditis, magna turba civium in forum convenit ad senatorem redeuntem exspectandum.
4   ubi urbe capta muri deleti erant, omnes ad portum festinavimus.
5   multis post annis, dum Romae habito, feminam olim conspectam iterum petere constitui.
6   pueri qui in via aderant adeo clamaverunt ut timerem ne ab imperatore audirentur.
7   paucis militibus missis ut portas custodirent, dux ceteris imperavit ut lente progrederentur.
8   postquam omnes epistulas a te scriptas legi, totam rem multo verius intellegebam.
9   servus qui vinum iam abstulerat deinde pecunia rapta e villa fugit ne a domino inveniretur.
10 ubi nomen huius regis audivi, sensi eum fratre interfecto crudeliorem futurum esse.

IMPORTANT WORDS WITH MORE THAN ONE MEANING

Some of these are alternative meanings of what is in origin the same word, others are homonyms (unrelated words coincidentally spelled in the same way).

				see page:
ad	(1)	to, towards, at	preposition with the accusative	61
	(2)	in order to	followed by gerundive	142
cum	(1)	with	preposition with the ablative	62
	(2)	when, since	introducing clause with subjunctive verb	152
hic	(1)	this	masculine nominative singular pronoun	48
	(2)	here	adverb	36
ne	(1)	not, not to	negative in purpose clause or indirect command	140, 145
	(2)	that	after verb of fearing	149
(-ne)	(3)	is it (etc)?	signals a question, attached to its first word	104
num	(1)	surely not?	in direct question	104
	(2)	whether	in indirect question	154–5
quam	(1)	how	in direct question or exclamation	105–6
	(2)	than	in comparison	29
	(3)	. . . as possible	with superlative adverb	38
	(4)	whom, which	feminine accusative singular of relative pronoun	54, 116
quod	(1)	because	introducing clause giving reason	113
	(2)	which	neuter nominative or accusative singular of relative pronoun	54, 116
ubi	(1)	when	introducing a time clause	111
	(2)	where	introducing a question or a clause explaining location	105, 106, 111

Note: *ubi* introducing a question is always *where*; in other contexts it can mean *when* or *where* (*quando* is used for *when* in a question).

ut	(1)	(in order) to	introducing a purpose clause	140
	(2)	to	introducing an indirect command	144
	(3)	that	introducing a result clause	146
	(4)	as	with indicative verb, or no verb	140

Exercise 71   Important words with more than one meaning (i)

1 servis imperavi ut celeriter laborarent.
2 servi celeriter laborabant ut laborem conficerent.
3 servi tam celeriter laborabant ut a domino saepe laudarentur.
4 servi, ut antea dixi, celeriter laborabant.
5 donum puellae misi quod tristissima esse videbatur.
6 donum quod puellae misi pulchrum erat.
7 senex fortior est quam iuvenis.
8 quam fortis es, amice!
9 quam graviter vulneratus est imperator?
10 ancilla quam heri vidi pulcherrima est.

Exercise 72   Important words with more than one meaning (ii)

1 milites tacebant ne ab hostibus invenirentur.
2 servis imperavi ne in horto clamarent.
3 cives timebant ne hostes urbem caperent.
4 tune haec scripsisti?
5 Romam cum fratre meo ire constitui.
6 cum frater meus domi manere mallet, Romam solus profectus sum.
7 servi, cum diu laboravissent, dormire volebant.
8 num illum librum legisti?
9 puerum rogavi num illum librum legisset.
10 puerone imperavisti ne illum librum legeret?

WORDS EASILY CONFUSED

absum	I am away	iaceo	I lie (down)
adsum	I am here	iacio	I throw
alter	the other (of two)	ita	in this way, so
altus	high, deep	itaque	and so, therefore
ante	before (*prep + acc*)	iter	journey
antea	before, previously	iterum	again
audeo	I dare	laetus	happy
audio	I hear	latus	having been carried
canem	dog (*acc*)	liber	book
cenam	dinner (*acc*)	liberi	children
		libero	I set free
capio	I take	libertus	freedman, ex-slave
cupio	I want		
		malo	I prefer
cena	dinner	malus	bad
cibus	food		
		maneo	I remain
cogito	I think	moneo	I warn
cognosco	I get to know		
cogo	I force	novem	nine
		novus	new
descendo	I go down		
discedo	I depart	oppugno	I attack
		pugno	I fight
dico	I say		
duco	I lead	porta	gate
		porto	I carry
domina	mistress	portus	harbour
dominus	master		
domus	house	post	after (*prep + acc*)
		postea	afterwards
forte	by chance	postquam	after (X *happened*, . . .)
fortis	brave, strong		
fortiter	bravely, strongly	posui	I placed
		potui	I was able
habeo	I have		
habito	I live	reddo	I give back
		redeo	I go back
hortor	I encourage	rideo	I laugh
hortus	garden		

res	thing (*acc* rem)	tamen	however
rex	king (*acc* regem)	tandem	at last
saepe	often	terreo	I frighten
semper	always	timeo	I fear
simul	at the same time	trado	I hand over
simulac	as soon as	traho	I drag
soleo	I am accustomed	via	road, way
solus	alone	vita	life
stat	he stands	vici	I conquered
statim	at once, immediately	vixi	I lived
subito	suddenly		
		vulnus	wound
summus	top (of)	vultus	face
sumus	we are		

Exercise 73   Words easily confused (i)

1 pueros de verbis quae cognoverant cogitare coegi.
2 ego diu aberam; libertus tamen qui aderat libros liberis tandem dedit.
3 a domino domum missus sum.
4 pater nos saepe hortabatur ut in horto semper maneremus.
5 hic puer semper redit, semper ridet; sed pecuniam saepe non reddit.
6 ego post portam iacebam, sed frater meus libros in portum postea iaciebat.
7 milites muros fortiter custodiebant sed ducem hostium forte non viderunt.
8 hic miles qui vulnus in vultu habet hic habitat.
9 summus mons ubi nunc sumus altior altero est.
10 malo omnia haec ipse trahere quam malo servo tradere.

Exercise 74   Words easily confused (ii)

1 milites fideles ubi dico omnia audiunt, ubi duco omnia audent.
2 dei soli omnia scire solent.
3 de monte cras descendam; deinde a patria discedam.
4 ancilla cibum emit ut cenam pararet.
5 nautae navem in flumen posuerunt, sed navigare non potuerunt.
6 via ad virtutem longa est sed vita brevis.
7 canem cenam meam consumentem inveni.
8 puer qui subito advenerat statim discessit.
9 putasne regem totam rem nunc scire?
10 imperator multos hostes vicit et multos annos vixit.

SUMMARY OF USES OF THE SUBJUNCTIVE

Expect to see an *imperfect* subjunctive (see page 138) in the following constructions:

purpose clause (see page 140)
Romam festinavimus ut imperatorem videremus.
We hurried to Rome to see the emperor.

indirect command (see page 144)
dominus servis imperavit ut celerius laborarent.
The master ordered the slaves to work more quickly.

result clause (see page 146)
puer tam stultus erat ut nihil intellegeret.
The boy was so stupid that he understood nothing.

clause after verb of fearing (see page 149)
cives timebant ne portus oppugnaretur.
The citizens were afraid that the harbour would be attacked.

time clause also expressing purpose (see page 143)
in foro manebam dum amici advenirent.
I was waiting in the forum for my friends to arrive.

cum *clause* (see page 152)
cum nullam pecuniam haberemus, miserrimi eramus.
Since we had no money, we were very miserable.

indirect question (see page 154)
puerum rogavi quid consumeret.
I asked the boy what he was eating.

Expect to see a *pluperfect* subjunctive (see page 150) in the following constructions:

cum *clause* (see page 152)
cum nihil audivissem, domi manebam.
Since I had heard nothing, I stayed at home.

indirect question (see page 154)
puellam rogavi quid fecisset.
I asked the girl what she had done.

Exercise 75   Uses of the subjunctive

1 pueri adeo clamabant ut verba mea audire non possent.
2 milites nostri semper fortiter pugnabant ut hostes vincerent.
3 pater filio imperavit ut statim rediret.
4 cives cognoscere conabantur num hostes fugissent.
5 cum via longissima esset, media nocte domum advenimus.
6 in foro manebamus dum nuntius rediret.
7 dominus servos rogavit quid ibi facerent.
8 puella timebat ne pecunia auferretur.
9 frater meus, cum tot praemia accepisset, laetissimus erat.
10 servus in silva se celavit ne a domino crudeli inveniretur.

APPENDIX: PRACTICE TRANSLATION PASSAGES

1 *The philosopher and mathematician Archimedes is tragically killed.*

Romani Syracusam primo navibus oppugnare conati sunt. deinde, quod urbem hoc modo capere non poterant, duos annos obsidebant. cives ubi tandem victi sunt nihil aliud quam salutem sibi liberisque rogaverunt; quae a Romanis promissa est. urbs tamen militibus data est ut praedam peterent.
5 multa tum irae exempla erant, multa avaritiae.

inter haec Archimedes philosophus interfectus est. nam inter tumultum urbis captae, miles Romanus domum quandam intravit ut aurum caperet. ibi hominem conspexit quem nesciebat. miles eum rogavit quis esset. philosophus tamen formas quas in pulvere scripserat inspiciebat. nihil
10 dixit. Romanus igitur ei imperavit ut statim responderet. sed Archimedes formis suis tam intentus erat ut verba militis non audiret. tum Romanus ira incensus nulla mora Graecum necavit. imperator tamen exercitus Romanorum, Marcellus nomine, quod mortem philosophi graviter tulit, militem severe puniri iussit.

Names

Syracusa -ae (*f*)	Syracuse (*a city in Sicily*)
Archimedes -is (*m*)	Archimedes
Graecus -i (*m*)	Greek, Greek man
Marcellus -i (*m*)	Marcellus

Vocabulary

obsideo -ere	I besiege
salus -utis (*f*)	safety
praeda -ae (*f*)	spoil, plunder
exemplum -i (*n*)	example
avaritia -ae (*f*)	greed
philosophus -i (*m*)	philosopher
tumultus -us (*m*)	commotion, uproar
aurum -i (*n*)	gold
forma -ae (*f*)	shape, diagram
pulvis -eris (*m*)	dust
inspicio -ere	I look at, I examine
intentus -a -um	intent
mora -ae (*f*)	delay
severe	severely

2 *Alexander the Great comes to power and describes his military ambitions.*

cum <u>Philippus</u> <u>Macedonum</u> rex ab inimico necatus esset, regnum <u>obtinuit</u>
<u>Alexander</u> filius eius, iuvenis tum <u>viginti</u> annos <u>natus</u>. hic statim in
pericula maxima venit: gentes enim a <u>Philippo</u> victae sperabant se
<u>rebellione</u> facta <u>libertatem</u> suam facile <u>recuperaturas esse</u>. <u>Alexander</u>
5   autem tam celeriter in hostium terram profectus est ut nemo resistere
posset et omnes sine proelio eum <u>victorem</u> salutarent.

deinde <u>Alexander</u> ducibus <u>Graecorum</u> <u>convocatis</u> nuntiavit se in <u>Asiam</u>
exercitum magnum ducturum esse ut <u>Dario</u> e regno expulso locum eius
ipse teneret. '<u>Achilles</u> olim' inquit 'e gente mea miles fortissimus, in <u>Asia</u>
10 <u>gloriam</u> bello accepit: cuius <u>exemplo</u> ego in <u>Asiam</u> profectus hos <u>barbaros</u>
puniam qui, tribus <u>incursionibus</u> in <u>Graeciam</u> factis, <u>maioribus</u> nostris
<u>iniurias</u> gravissimas fecerunt.' quae cum dixisset, <u>Graeci</u> magno clamore
sublato <u>Alexandrum</u> laudaverunt et se copias ei daturos esse promiserunt.

Names

Philippus -i (*m*)	Philip
Macedones -um (*m pl*)	Macedonians
Alexander -dri (*m*)	Alexander
Graeci -orum (*m pl*)	Greeks
Asia -ae (*f*)	Asia
Darius -i (*m*)	Darius
Achilles -is (*m*)	Achilles
Graecia -ae (*f*)	Greece

Vocabulary

obtineo -ere -ui	I succeed to, I take over
viginti	twenty
natus -a -um	old, aged
rebellio -onis (*f*)	rebellion
libertas -atis (*f*)	freedom
recupero -are -avi -atus	I get (something) back
victor -oris (*m*)	victor, winner
convoco -are -avi -atus	I call together
gloria -ae (*f*)	glory
exemplum -i (*n*)	example
barbari -orum (*m pl*)	barbarians
incursio -onis (*f*)	invasion
maiores -um (*m pl*)	ancestors
iniuria -ae (*f*)	injustice

3 *Damocles learns that the life of a tyrant is less enviable than he thought.*

> Dionysius erat tyrannus Syracusanorum. cives eum tyrannum fecerant
> quod hostes suos vicerat. comes quidam Damocles nomine saepe
> loquebatur de imperio atque divitiis tyranni, cuius vitam laetissimam esse
> credebat. itaque Dionysius 'visne igitur' inquit 'hanc vitam, quod tibi ita
> 5 placet, ipse degustare?' cum Damocles dixisset se hoc cupere, Dionysius
> eum ad cenam magnificam invitavit.
>
> mensae cibo optimo gravissimae erant et vinum optimum liberaliter
> fundebatur. sed super lectum ubi Damocles recumbebat Dionysius gladium
> ingentem posuerat ut capiti eius impenderet. filum quod gladium tenebat
> 10 tenuissimum erat. itaque Damocles, timens ne subito necaretur, per totam
> cenam gladium intente spectabat. adeo timebat ut cibum consumere non
> posset, vinum bibere nollet. tyrannum igitur tandem oravit ut sibi domum
> redire permitteret, cum vitam eius habere iam nollet. intellexit enim
> tyrannum nihil gaudii habere cum metus ei semper impenderet.

Names

Dionysius -i (*m*)	Dionysius
Syracusani -orum (*m pl*)	Syracusans, people of Syracuse (*a city in Sicily*)
Damocles -is (*m*)	Damocles

Vocabulary

tyrannus -i (*m*)	tyrant, ruler
divitiae -arum (*f pl*)	riches, wealth
placeo -ere	I am pleasing
degusto -are	I have a taste of
magnificus -a -um	magnificent
mensa -ae (*f*)	table
liberaliter	generously
fundo -ere	I pour
lectus -i (*m*)	couch
recumbo -ere	I recline
impendo -ere	I hang over (+ *dat*)
filum -i (*n*)	thread
tenuis -e	thin
intente	intently
permitto -ere	I allow (+ *dat*)
metus -us (*m*)	fear

4 *King Tarquinius buys some unusual books.*

anus incognita ad Tarquinium Superbum regem adiit. novem libros ferebat
quos oracula deorum esse dicebat. libros vendere volebat, sed tantam
pecuniam postulavit ut rex ridens anum insanam esse crederet. deinde illa
ad focum ambulavit et tres libros in ignem iniecit. his deletis, Tarquinium
5 rogavit num libros reliquos eodem pretio emere vellet. illi tamen non
persuasit: rex multo magis risit. itaque anus tres alios libros statim incendit.
quod cum fecisset, placide rogavit num tres reliquos eodem pretio
empturus esset.

Tarquinius tandem, quod intellexit se tantam constantiam neglegere non
10 posse, anui paruit. libros igitur tres emit non minore pretio quam pro
omnibus primo petitum erat. et illa cum a rege discessisset postea
numquam visa est. libri tres, in templo positi, diligenter custodiebantur.
consilium eorum semper petebatur ubi populus Romanus de periculo
liberari debebat.

Names

Tarquinius -i Superbus -i (*m*)   Tarquinius Superbus (*also called just
Tarquinius*)

Vocabulary

anus -us (*f*)	old woman
incognitus -a -um	unknown
oraculum -i (*n*)	oracle, prophecy
postulo -are -avi	I demand
insanus -a -um	insane, mad
focus -i (*m*)	hearth
ignis -is (*m*)	fire
reliquus -a -um	remaining
pretium -i (*n*)	price
placide	calmly
constantia -ae (*f*)	perseverance
neglego -ere	I disregard
pareo -ere	I obey (+ *dat*)
populus -i (*m*)	people

5 *Lucretia is shamefully treated but remains noble to the end.*

Roma regebatur a rege <u>superbo</u>, cuius filius erat <u>Sextus Tarquinius</u>.
quadam nocte cum <u>Tarquinius</u> et amici vinum biberent, coeperunt uxores
suas laudare. <u>Collatinus</u> dixit suam <u>Lucretiam</u> optimam esse. 'quid creditis
eam nunc facere?' inquit 'ego vos ad villam meam ducam. tum videbitis
5 eam meliorem esse ceteris.' hoc omnibus <u>placuit</u>. cum ad villam
advenissent, <u>Lucretiam</u> non <u>ludentem</u> sed <u>lanam ducentem</u> invenerunt.
<u>Sextus</u> tamen, cum videret quam pulchra <u>Lucretia</u> esset, amore scelesto
captus est.

paucis post diebus, cum abesset <u>Collatinus</u>, ille regressus <u>cubiculum</u>
10 <u>Lucretiae</u> intravit. 'tace!' inquit '<u>Sextus Tarquinius</u> sum. gladium in manu
fero. <u>aut cede</u> mihi <u>aut</u> te necabo!' quamquam <u>Lucretia</u> dixit se necari
malle, <u>Sextus</u> tandem <u>pudicitiam</u> eius vicit. tum discessit. <u>Collatinus</u>, cum
omnia audivisset, <u>iuravit</u> se <u>Sextum</u> puniturum esse. <u>Lucretia</u>, ne aliis
uxoribus malum <u>exemplum</u> esse videretur, se necavit. 'ego me non <u>culpo</u>,
sed poena non libero' moriens dixit.

Names

Sextus -i Tarquinius -i (*m*)	Sextus Tarquinius (*called by either or both names*)
Collatinus -i (*m*)	Collatinus
Lucretia -ae (*f*)	Lucretia

Vocabulary

superbus -a -um	proud, arrogant
placeo -ere -ui	I am pleasing
ludo -ere	I play
lanam duco -ere	I spin wool
cubiculum -i (*n*)	bedroom
aut . . . aut	either . . . or
cedo -ere	I yield, I give way
pudicitia -ae (*f*)	modesty, virtue
iuro -are -avi	I swear
exemplum -i (*n*)	example
culpo -are	I blame

6 *Horatius defends the single bridge over the Tiber from enemy attack.*

nemo praeter duos comites, viros audaces, cum Horatio nunc manebat.
ceteris pontem a tergo gladio et igne delere iussis, periculum impetus cum
his primo ferebat. deinde, cum parva pars pontis maneret, comites in locum
tutum abire coegit. Horatius, qui antea promiserat se urbem servaturum
5   esse, in ponte solus contra multos stabat. duces hostium saevissime
spectabat ut ad pugnam provocaret. tot hostes iam interfecerat ut ceteri
primo progredi timerent. sed tandem illi magno cum clamore tela in unum
Romanum iecerunt.

Horatius magna virtute se scuto defendebat. subito tamen, ponte tandem
10   rupto, clamorem suorum audivit. tum Horatius, multis vulneribus acceptis,
deo fluminis precatus est. 'Tiberine pater' inquit 'accipe hunc militem et
haec arma flumine tuo.' deinde in aquam desiluit armatus. quamquam
multa tela ab hostibus iaciebantur, ad alteram ripam tutus tranavit.

Names

Horatius -i (*m*)	Horatius
Tiberinus -i (*m*)	Tiberinus (*god of the Tiber*)

Vocabulary

praeter	except (+ *acc*)
pons pontis (*m*)	bridge
tergum -i (*n*)	back
ignis -is (*m*)	fire
impetus -us (*m*)	attack
tutus -a -um	safe
pugna -ae (*f*)	fight
provoco -are	I provoke, I challenge
telum -i (*n*)	weapon, missile
scutum -i (*n*)	shield
desilio -ire -ui	I jump down
armatus -a -um	fully armed
ripa -ae (*f*)	bank
trano -are -avi	I swim across

7   *Menenius Agrippa gives advice by telling a story.*

olim erat inter Romanos magna <u>discordia</u>. milites enim cum ducibus suis
<u>parere</u> nollent ex urbe in montem quendam discesserant. cives igitur
perterriti <u>Menenium Agrippam</u>, virum sapientem militibusque <u>carum</u>, ad
eos reducendos miserunt. ille, ubi in montem venit, <u>fabulam</u> eis narravit.

5   'olim erat in corpore magna <u>discordia</u>. partes enim corporis <u>ventrem</u>
magno clamore simul <u>culpabant</u>. omnes dixerunt <u>ventrem</u> cibum suo labore
datum semper consumere sed ipsum in medio sedentem nihil facere. itaque
manus "cibum" inquit "ad <u>os</u> non portabo". <u>os</u> dixit se cibum accipere
nolle, <u>dentes</u>que "nos" inquiunt "cibum non <u>manducabimus</u>". <u>venter</u> igitur
10   cum cibum non haberet in magno periculo mox erat. non tamen <u>ventrem</u>
vicerunt partes corporis, sed ipsae in periculum mortis venerunt. nam
sanguinem, quem <u>venter</u> corpori <u>praebet</u>, sine auxilio eius non habuerunt.'
<u>Agrippa</u> igitur his verbis militibus persuasit ut in urbem regrederentur.

Names

Menenius -i Agrippa -ae (*m*)	Menenius Agrippa (*also called just Agrippa*)

Vocabulary

discordia -ae (*f*)	disagreement
pareo -ere	I obey (+ *dat*)
carus -a -um	dear
fabula -ae (*f*)	story
venter -tris (*m*)	stomach
culpo -are	I blame
os oris (*n*)	mouth
dens dentis (*m*)	tooth
manduco -are	I chew
praebeo -ere	I provide

8 *Coriolanus is forced to change his mind about attacking his own city.*

Coriolanus qui dux Romanorum fuerat a populo suo expulsus est. ab urbe
fugit ad Volscos qui illo tempore bellum contra Romanos gerebant.
feminae igitur Romanae, quod timebant ne Coriolanus patriam oppugnaret,
ad matrem uxoremque eius venerunt. quibus persuaserunt ut secum ad
5   castra hostium adirent. feminae enim sperabant se urbem, cum armis
defendere non possent, precibus lacrimisque servaturas esse.

cum ad castra pervenissent amicus quidam Coriolano nuntiavit magnam
turbam feminarum adesse. ille primo quaerere noluit quid vellent. deinde
amicus, qui illas cognoverat, 'nisi oculi me decipiunt' inquit 'mater tua et
10 uxor adsunt, cum duobus parvis filiis.' tum Coriolanus surrexit ad eas
salutandas. sed mater irata rogavit utrum ad filium an ad hostem venisset,
utrum captiva an mater in castris eius esset. quibus verbis permotus
Coriolanus exercitum ab urbe movit sed postea a Volscis interfectus est.

Names

Coriolanus -i (*m*)	Coriolanus
Volsci -orum (*m pl*)	Volscians

Vocabulary

populus -i (*m*)	people
secum	= cum se
preces -ium (*f pl*)	prayers
lacrima -ae (*f*)	tear
oculus -i (*m*)	eye
decipio -ere	I deceive
utrum . . . an	whether . . . or
captiva -ae (*f*)	(female) prisoner
permotus -a -um	moved, affected

9   *Manlius Torquatus puts his duty as a general above his feelings as a father.*

dum Romani contra <u>Latinos</u> pugnant, <u>Manlius Torquatus</u> exercitum
ducebat; filius eius, <u>Titus</u> nomine, <u>equitibus</u> <u>praeerat</u>. <u>Torquatus</u>, vir
<u>severus</u> sed <u>pugna</u> fortissimus, militibus suis imperavit ne extra <u>ordinem</u>
irent ut cum hostibus pugnarent. <u>disciplinam</u> enim exercitus hoc modo
5 <u>augere</u> volebat. <u>Titus</u> tamen prope <u>stationem</u> quandam <u>Latinorum</u> aderat.
ibi <u>Geminus Minucius</u>, <u>equitum</u> hostium dux, ridens dixit eum <u>secum</u>
pugnare timere. <u>Titus</u> igitur tam iratus erat ut, verborum patris <u>oblitus</u>,
illum saevissime oppugnatum necavit et arma cepit.

ubi in castra rediit, arma <u>Minucii</u> patri statim dedit. <u>Torquatus</u> tamen
10 vultum a filio <u>avertit</u> et '<u>Tite Manli</u>' inquit 'quod neque imperatori neque
patri <u>paruisti</u>, te interfici iubeo'. his verbis dictis omnes milites miseri
erant. <u>Torquatum</u> enim ferocius egisse credebant quam deberet. sed ex illo
tempore ei semper <u>parebant</u> et <u>officia</u> sua diligentius faciebant. <u>Latinis</u>
igitur hoc anno superatis, <u>Torquatus</u> a militibus laudatus est.

Names

Latini -orum (*m pl*)	Latins, people of Latium
Manlius -i Torquatus -i (*m*)	Manlius Torquatus (*also called just Torquatus*)
Titus -i (*m*)	Titus (*also called Titus Manlius*)
Geminus -i Minucius -i (*m*)	Geminus Minucius

Vocabulary

equites -um (*m pl*)	cavalry
praesum -esse	I am in charge of (+ *dat*)
severus -a -um	strict
pugna -ae (*f*)	fight, fighting
ordo -inis (*m*)	line
disciplina -ae (*f*)	discipline
augeo -ere	I increase (something)
statio -onis (*f*)	outpost
secum	= cum se
obliviscor -i oblitus sum	I forget (+ *gen*)
averto -ere -i	I turn (something) away
pareo -ere -ui	I obey (+ *dat*)
officium -i (*n*)	job, duty

10 *Papirius finds a way of dealing with his mother's curiosity.*

mos antea erat senatoribus Romanis in curiam cum filiis intrare. ubi olim
res magna de qua senatores consulebant in posterum diem prolata est,
mater Papirii pueri qui cum patre in curia fuerat filium rogavit quid
senatores agerent. omnes tamen qui in curia aderant de hac re tacere iussi
5   erant. itaque puer respondit se nihil dicturum esse. mater tamen iterum
atque iterum rogavit.

tandem igitur Papirius lepidam fabulam excogitavit. dixit enim senatores
consulere utrum unus vir duas uxores habere deberet, an una femina duos
maritos. quod cum mater audivisset, domo statim egressa aliis feminis
10   nuntiavit quid filius dixisset. illae igitur omnes ad curiam festinaverunt.
cum advenissent orabant senatores ut una femina duos maritos haberet.
quae verba audita senatores mirati sunt quod nesciebant cur feminae ita
postularent. tum puer Papirius surrexit et omnibus narravit quid mater
rogavisset, quidque ipse matri dixisset.

Name

Papirius -i (*m*)   Papirius

Vocabulary

mos moris (*m*)   custom
curia -ae (*f*)   senate-house
consulo -ere   I have a discussion
posterus -a -um   next, following
profero -ferre -tuli -latus   I postpone, I defer
lepidus -a -um   charming, witty
fabula -ae (*f*)   story
excogito -are -avi   I think up, I invent
utrum . . . an   whether . . . or
postulo -are   I demand

11 *Hannibal has a dream about his planned invasion of Italy.*

Hannibal in Hispania contra socios Romanorum bellum gerebat. Romani enim ipsi hostes eius diu fuerant. cum urbem Saguntum cepisset, exercitum in Italiam ducere constituit ut Romam oppugnaret. ea nocte in somnio videbatur in concilium deorum vocari. ibi Hannibali, roganti quid facere
5 deberet, Iuppiter imperavit ut quam celerrime proficisceretur. rex deorum promisit se ei daturum esse ducem qui exercitum eius in Italiam duceret. hic dux Hannibali in eodem somnio apparuit et 'noli' inquit 'in itinere oculos revertere'.

ille tamen, non longe progressus, cum milites suos in campo instructos
10 videre cuperet, duci non paruit. tum a tergo conspexit monstrum ingens, quod omnes arbores et plurima aedificia delebat. cum Hannibal miratus quaesivisset quid significaret tantum monstrum, dux respondet vastitatem Italiae esse. eum hortatus est ne curaret quid a tergo faceretur sed Italiam quam celerrime peteret.

Names

Hannibal -alis (*m*)	Hannibal
Hispania -ae (*f*)	Spain
Saguntum -i (*n*)	Saguntum (*a city in Spain*)
Italia -ae (*f*)	Italy
Iuppiter (*m*)	Jupiter

Vocabulary

socius -i (*m*)	ally
somnium -i (*n*)	dream
concilium -i (*n*)	assembly, meeting
oculus -i (*m*)	eye
campus -i (*m*)	plain
instruo -ere -xi -ctus	I draw up, I arrange
pareo -ere -ui	I obey (+ *dat*)
tergum -i (*n*)	back
monstrum -i (*n*)	monster
arbor -oris (*f*)	tree
aedificium -i (*n*)	building
significo -are	I mean, I signify
vastitas -atis (*f*)	devastation, destruction
curo -are	I care

12   *Regulus puts the interests of Rome before his own.*

tum <u>Regulus</u> dux, quem <u>Carthaginienses</u> ceperant, Romam missus est ut
pacem ab eis peteret et <u>permutationem</u> captivorum faceret. cum ad urbem
advenisset, amici gaudentes eum in <u>curiam</u> duxerunt. sed <u>Regulus</u> nihil
<u>quasi</u> Romanus egit. dixit enim se, ex illo die ubi in <u>potestatem</u> hostium
5 venisset, civem Romanum esse <u>desivisse</u>. itaque senatoribus persuasit ne
pax cum <u>Carthaginiensibus</u> faceretur. dixit enim hostes multis <u>cladibus</u>
confectos spem nullam habere. noluit plurimos eorum captivos reddi pro se
et paucis Romanis captis.

amici <u>Regulo</u> persuadere conati sunt ne <u>Carthaginem</u> rediret. uxorem igitur
10 eius et filios ad <u>curiam</u> invitaverunt. illa liberos marito ostendens oravit ut
domi maneret. <u>Regulus</u> tamen dixit se malle hostibus tradi. deinde
<u>Carthaginem</u> rediit, quamquam sciebat hostes se necaturos esse. Romani
hostes pacem petentes accipere noluerunt. sic <u>Regulus</u> summum <u>fidei</u>
virtutisque <u>exemplum</u> omnibus qui aderant <u>praebuit</u>.

Names

Regulus -i (*m*)	Regulus
Carthaginienses -ium (*m pl*)	Carthaginians
Carthago -inis (*f*)	Carthage (*a city in North Africa*)

Vocabulary

permutatio -onis (*f*)	exchange
curia -ae (*f*)	senate-house
quasi	like, as
potestas -atis (*f*)	power
desino -ere desivi	I cease
clades -is (*f*)	disaster
fides -ei (*f*)	loyalty
exemplum -i (*n*)	example
praebeo -ere -ui	I provide

13 *A murder is revealed by dreams.*

duo iuvenes iter per <u>Graeciam</u> olim faciebant. cum <u>Megaram</u> venissent,
alter in taberna alter apud amicum <u>pernoctavit</u>. dum <u>hic</u> dormit, <u>ille</u>
apparere visus est et orare ut <u>adiuvaret</u>, cum mors sibi a <u>caupone</u> pararetur.
is <u>somnio</u> perterritus statim surrexit. mox tamen, ubi intellexit se sine <u>causa</u>
5   timere, iterum dormivit.

tum ei dormienti <u>umbra</u> amici iterum apparuit. 'occisus sum' inquit 'quod
tu nihil fecisti. sed quamquam me vivum non <u>adiuvisti</u>, mortuum <u>vindica</u>.
<u>caupo</u> ille scelestus puniri debet. nolo eum effugere posse.' dixit se
interfectum in <u>plaustrum</u> iactum esse <u>fimo</u> <u>supra</u> iniecto. petivit ut amicus
10   prima luce ad portam <u>oppidi</u> adesset. 'hoc modo' inquit '<u>plaustrum</u> exire
non poterit.' quibus verbis <u>commotus</u> amicus surrexit et ad portam <u>oppidi</u>
festinavit. servum conspectum rogavit quid in <u>plaustro</u> esset. ille
perterritus fugit, sed corpore invento <u>caupo</u> poenas dedit.

Names

Graecia -ae (*f*)	Greece
Megara -ae (*f*)	Megara (*a town in Greece*)

Vocabulary

pernocto -are -avi	I spend the night
hic . . . ille	the latter . . . the former
adiuvo -are -i	I help
caupo -onis (*m*)	innkeeper
somnium -i (*n*)	dream
causa -ae (*f*)	reason, cause
umbra -ae (*f*)	ghost
vindico -are	I avenge, I obtain vengeance for
plaustrum -i (*n*)	wagon, cart
fimus -i (*m*)	manure
supra	on top
oppidum -i (*n*)	town
commotus -a -um	disturbed

14 *A band of robbers recruit a new leader, with unexpected results.*

olim <u>latrones</u> <u>oppidum</u> oppugnaverunt et puellam pulchram ceperunt. quam
cum duxissent ad <u>speluncam</u> in qua habitabant, ibi <u>captivam</u> tenebant.
puella tristissima erat, quod amicum habebat, qui se <u>in matrimonium</u>
<u>ducere</u> cupiebat. postquam dux <u>latronum</u> in <u>impetu</u> necatus est, ceteri
5   novum ducem quaerere constituerunt. paucis post diebus iuvenem
quendam, <u>Haemum</u> nomine, invenerunt. quod fortissimus esse videbatur,
eum primum oraverunt ut <u>latro</u> fieret, deinde principem fecerunt.

interea de puella <u>consuluerunt</u>: alii eam ancillam esse volebant, alii
interficere ne <u>molesta</u> esset. <u>Haemus</u> autem eis persuasit ut puellam in
10   urbem ductam magno <u>pretio</u> vendere conarentur. puella, simulac se non
iam morituram esse cognovit, laetissima fuit. illa nocte <u>Haemus</u> cena
parata tantum vini <u>latronibus</u> dedit ut brevi tempore omnes dormirent. ipse
tamen neque vinum bibit neque dormivit, sed <u>latronibus</u> <u>vinctis</u> puellam
domum reduxit. <u>latrones</u> enim nesciebant <u>Haemum</u> <u>sponsum</u> puellae esse.

Name

Haemus -i (*m*)   Haemus

Vocabulary

latro -onis (*m*)   robber
oppidum -i (*n*)   town
spelunca -ae (*f*)   cave
captiva -ae (*f*)   (female) prisoner
in matrimonium duco   I marry
impetus -us (*m*)   raid, attack
consulo -ere -ui   I consult, I have a discussion
molestus -a -um   troublesome
pretium -i (*n*)   price
vincio -ire vinxi vinctus   I tie (someone) up
sponsus -i (*m*)   fiancé

15 *Mycerinus finds a way to cheat the gods.*

Mycerinus, ut dicitur, rex Aegyptiorum factus, nuntios ad oraculum Iovis
misit, cum a deo cognoscere vellet quot annos victurus esset. deus
respondit Mycerinum, cum sex annos rexisset, subito periturum esse. quae
verba miratus ille 'dei me decipiunt' inquit 'nam pater et avunculus meus,
5 qui populum multis iniuriis opprimebant, diu vixerunt; mihi tamen bene et
fideliter regenti Iuppiter vitam brevissimam dedit.'

tum nuntiis imperavit ut ad oraculum iterum irent et a deo peterent cur
pietas sua ita puniretur. illi regressi nuntiaverunt deum iratum esse, cum
ipse constituisset Aegyptios centum annos crudelia passuros esse. itaque
10 Mycerinus, cum se diu victurum esse non iam speraret, multas lucernas
paravit ut per noctes, sicut per dies, conviviis sine fine frueretur. 'hoc
modo' inquit 'ego deos decipiam et sex annos ab eis mihi datos sic
duplicabo.'

Names

Mycerinus -i (*m*)	Mycerinus
Aegyptii -orum (*m pl*)	Egyptians
Iupiter Iovis (*m*)	Jupiter

Vocabulary

oraculum -i (*n*)	oracle
victurus -a -um	going to live (*future participle of* vivo)
decipio -ere	I cheat (someone)
avunculus -i (*m*)	uncle
iniuria -ae (*f*)	injury, injustice
pietas -atis (*f*)	dutiful behaviour
lucerna -ae (*f*)	lamp
sicut	just as, just like
convivium -i (*n*)	feast
finis -is (*m*)	end
fruor -i	I enjoy (+ *abl*)
decipio -ere	I cheat (someone)
duplico -are	I double

VOCABULARY

The second column has further information about each word:

• Verbs are shown with principal parts (see page 77): present tense (first person singular) in the first column, then infinitive (showing conjugation, e.g. 3rd), perfect tense (first person singular), and perfect passive participle. Note that 3rd* = mixed 3rd/4th conjugation: these verbs count as 3rd because of infinitive *-ere*, but form present, imperfect and future tenses like 4th (see page 68).

• Nouns are shown with genitive singular, gender, and declension (e.g. 3).

• Adjectives are given with feminine and neuter. If only one other form is given, it is the neuter (and the feminine is the same as the masculine). Third declension adjectives of the *ingens* type (see page 26) are shown instead with the genitive singular (for the stem).

• Common irregular forms are cross-referenced.

• For explanation of abbreviations, see the list on page x.

a/ab	+ *abl, or as prefix*	*prep*	from, away from, by
abstuli		(*perfect of* aufero)	
absum	abesse, afui	*verb irreg*	be absent, be away, be distant from
ac/atque	*indecl*	*conj*	and
accepi		(*perfect of* accipio)	
accido	accidere, accidi	*verb 3rd*	happen
accipio	accipere, accepi, acceptus	*verb 3rd**	accept, take in, receive
actus	acta, actum	(*perfect passive participle of* ago)	
ad	+ *acc, or as prefix*	*prep*	to, towards, at
adeo	*indecl*	*adv*	so much, so greatly
adsum	adesse, adfui	*verb irreg*	be here, be present
advenio	advenire, adveni	*verb 4th*	arrive
aedifico	aedificare, aedificavi, aedificatus	*verb 1st*	build
ager	agri	*noun m 2*	field
ago	agere, egi, actus	*verb 3rd*	do, act, drive
alius	alia, aliud	*adj/pron*	other, another, else
alii . . . alii			some . . . others (*see page 59*)
alter	altera, alterum	*adj/pron*	the other, another, the second of two
alter . . . alter			one . . . the other (*see page 59*)
altus	alta, altum	*adj*	high, deep

ambulo	ambulare, ambulavi	*verb 1st*	walk
amicus	amici	*noun m 2*	friend
amo	amare, amavi, amatus	*verb 1st*	love, like
amor	amoris	*noun m 3*	love
ancilla	ancillae	*noun f 1*	slave-girl, slave-woman
animus	animi	*noun m 2*	mind, spirit, soul
annus	anni	*noun m 2*	year
ante	*+ acc*	*prep*	before, in front of
antea	*indecl*	*adv*	before, previously
appareo	apparere, apparui	*verb 2nd*	appear
appropinquo	appropinquare, appropinquavi	*verb 1st*	approach, come near to (*usu + dat*)
apud	*+ acc*	*prep*	among, with, at the house of
aqua	aquae	*noun f 1*	water
arma	armorum	*noun n 2 pl*	arms, weapons
ars	artis	*noun f 3*	art, skill
ascendo	ascendere, ascendi, ascensus	*verb 3rd*	climb
audax	*gen* audacis	*adj*	bold, daring
audeo	audere, ausus sum	*verb 2nd s-dep*	dare
audio	audire, audivi, auditus	*verb 4th*	hear, listen to
aufero	auferre, abstuli, ablatus	*verb irreg*	take away, carry off, steal
autem	*indecl*	*conj*	however, but
auxilium	auxilii	*noun n 2*	help
bellum	belli	*noun n 2*	war
bellum gero			wage war, campaign
bene	*indecl*	*adv*	well
benignus	benigna, benignum	*adj*	kind
bibo	bibere, bibi	*verb 3rd*	drink
bonus	bona, bonum	*adj*	good
melior	melius	*adj*	better
optimus	optima, optimum	*adj*	best, excellent, very good
brevis	breve	*adj*	short, brief
cado	cadere, cecidi	*verb 3rd*	fall
caelum	caeli	*noun n 2*	sky, heaven
canis	canis	*noun m/f 3*	dog
capio	capere, cepi, captus	*verb 3rd**	take, catch, capture
captivus	captivi	*noun m 2*	captive, prisoner
captus	capta, captum	(*perfect passive participle of* capio)	
caput	capitis	*noun n 3*	head
castra	castrorum	*noun n 2 pl*	camp
cecidi		(*perfect of* cado)	
celer	celeris, celere	*adj*	quick, fast
celo	celare, celavi, celatus	*verb 1st*	hide

cena	cenae	*noun f 1*	dinner, meal
centum	*indecl*	*num*	100
cepi		*(perfect of* capio)	
ceteri	ceterae, cetera	*adj/pron*	the rest, the others
cibus	cibi	*noun m 2*	food
circum	*+ acc*	*prep*	around
civis	civis	*noun m/f 3*	citizen
clamo	clamare, clamavi, clamatus	*verb 1st*	shout
clamor	clamoris	*noun m 3*	shout, shouting, noise
clarus	clara, clarum	*adj*	famous, clear
coactus	coacta, coactum	*(perfect passive participle of* cogo)	
coegi		*(perfect of* cogo)	
coepi	coepisse, coeptus	*verb irreg*	began *(perfect: see page 90)*
cogito	cogitare, cogitavi, cogitatus	*verb 1st*	think, consider
cognosco	cognoscere, cognovi, cognitus	*verb 3rd*	get to know, find out
cogo	cogere, coegi, coactus	*verb 3rd*	force, compel
comes	comitis	*noun m/f 3*	companion, comrade
conficio	conficere, confeci, confectus	*verb 3rd**	finish; wear out
conor	conari, conatus sum	*verb 1st dep*	try
consilium	consilii	*noun n 2*	plan, idea, advice
conspectus	conspecta, conspectum	*(perfect passive participle of* conspicio)	
conspexi		*(perfect of* conspicio)	
conspicio	conspicere, conspexi, conspectus	*verb 3rd**	catch sight of, notice
constituo	constituere, constitui, constitutus	*verb 3rd*	decide
consul	consulis	*noun m 3*	consul
consumo	consumere, consumpsi, consumptus	*verb 3rd*	eat
contra	*+ acc*	*prep*	against
convenio	convenire, conveni, conventus	*verb 4th*	come together, gather, meet
copiae	copiarum	*noun f 1 pl*	forces, troops
corpus	corporis	*noun n 3*	body
cras	*indecl*	*adv*	tomorrow
credo	credere, credidi, creditus	*verb 3rd*	believe, trust (+ *dat*)
crudelis	crudele	*adj*	cruel
cucurri		*(perfect of* curro)	
cum	*indecl*	*conj*	when, since
cum	*+ abl*	*prep*	with
cupio	cupere, cupivi, cupitus	*verb 3rd**	want, desire
cur?	*indecl*	*adv*	why?

cura	curae	*noun 1 f*	care, worry
curro	currere, cucurri, cursus	*verb 3rd*	run
custodio	custodire, custodivi, custoditus	*verb 4th*	guard
custos	custodis	*noun m/f 3*	guard
datus	data, datum	(*perfect passive participle of* do)	
de	+ *abl*	*prep*	from, down from; about
dea	deae	*noun f 1*	goddess
debeo	debere, debui, debitus	*verb 2nd*	owe, ought, should, must
decem	*indecl*	*num*	ten
dedi		(*perfect of* do)	
defendo	defendere, defendi, defensus	*verb 3rd*	defend
deicio	deicere, deieci, deiectus	*verb 3rd**	throw down
deinde	*indecl*	*adv*	then, next
deleo	delere, delevi, deletus	*verb 2nd*	destroy
descendo	descendere, descendi, descensus	*verb 3rd*	go down, come down
deus	dei	*noun m 2*	god
dico	dicere, dixi, dictus	*verb 3rd*	say
dies	diei	*noun m/f 5*	day
difficilis	difficile	*adj*	difficult
diligens	*gen* diligentis	*adj*	careful
dirus	dira, dirum	*adj*	dreadful
discedo	discedere, discessi	*verb 3rd*	depart, leave
diu	*indecl*	*adv*	for a long time
dixi		(*perfect of* dico)	
do	dare, dedi, datus	*verb 1st*	give
poenas do			pay the penalty, be punished
doceo	docere, docui, doctus	*verb 2nd*	teach
domina	dominae	*noun f 1*	mistress
dominus	domini	*noun m 2*	master
domus	domus (domi = at home)	*noun f 4*	house, home
donum	doni	*noun n 2*	gift, present
dormio	dormire, dormivi	*verb 4th*	sleep
duco	ducere, duxi, ductus	*verb 3rd*	lead, take
dum	*indecl*	*conj*	while, until
duo	duae, duo	*num*	two
dux	ducis	*noun m 3*	leader
duxi		(*perfect of* duco)	
e/ex	+ *abl, or as prefix*	*prep*	from, out of, out
ecce!	*indecl*	*interjection*	look! see!
effugio	effugere, effugi	*verb 3rd**	escape
egi		(*perfect of* ago)	
ego	mei	*pron*	I, me

egredior	egredi, egressus sum	*verb 3rd* dep*	go out
eicio	eicere, eieci, eiectus	*verb 3rd*	throw out
emo	emere, emi, emptus	*verb 3rd*	buy
enim	*indecl*	*conj*	for
eo	ire, i(v)i	*verb irreg*	go
epistula	epistulae	*noun f 1*	letter
equus	equi	*noun m 2*	horse
erumpo	erumpere, erupi, eruptus	*verb 3rd*	burst out
et	*indecl*	*conj*	and
et . . . et		both . . . and	
etiam	*indecl*	*adv*	also, even
eunt-		(*stem of present participle of* eo)	
exercitus	exercitus	*noun m 4*	army
expello	expellere, expuli, expulsus	*verb 3rd*	drive out
exspecto	exspectare, exspectavi, exspectatus	*verb 1st*	wait for
facilis	facile	*adj*	easy
facio	facere, feci, factus	*verb 3rd**	make, do
faveo	favere, favi	*verb 2nd*	favour, support (+ *dat*)
feci		(*perfect of* facio)	
felix	*gen* felicis	*adj*	fortunate, happy
femina	feminae	*noun f 1*	woman
fero	ferre, tuli, latus	*verb irreg*	bring, carry, bear
ferox	*gen* ferocis	*adj*	fierce, ferocious
festino	festinare, festinavi	*verb 1st*	hurry
fidelis	fidele	*adj*	faithful, loyal
filia	filiae	*noun f 1*	daughter
filius	filii	*noun m 2*	son
flumen	fluminis	*noun n 3*	river
forte	*indecl*	*adv*	by chance
fortis	forte	*adj*	brave
forum	fori	*noun n 2*	forum, marketplace
frater	fratris	*noun m 3*	brother
frustra	*indecl*	*adv*	in vain
fugio	fugere, fugi	*verb 3rd**	run away, flee
fui		(*perfect of* sum)	
futurus	futura, futurum	(*future participle of* sum)	
gaudeo	gaudere, gavisus sum	*verb 2nd s-dep*	rejoice, be pleased
gaudium	gaudii	*noun n 2*	joy, pleasure
gens	gentis	*noun f 3*	family, tribe, race, people
gero	gerere, gessi, gestus	*verb 3rd*	wage (war)
bellum gero			wage war, campaign
gladius	gladii	*noun m 2*	sword
gravis	grave	*adj*	heavy, serious

habeo	habere, habui, habitus	*verb 2nd*	have
habito	habitare, habitavi, habitatus	*verb 1st*	live, dwell
heri	*indecl*	*adv*	yesterday
hic	haec, hoc	*pron/adj*	this; he, she, it
hic	*indecl*	*adv*	here
hodie	*indecl*	*adv*	today
homo	hominis	*noun m 3*	man, human being
hora	horae	*noun f 1*	hour
hortor	hortari, hortatus sum	*verb 1st dep*	encourage, urge
hortus	horti	*noun m 2*	garden
hostis	hostis	*noun m 3*	enemy
iaceo	iacere, iacui	*verb 2nd*	lie
iacio	iacere, ieci, iactus	*verb 3rd**	throw
eicio	eicere, eieci, eiectus	*verb 3rd**	throw out
inicio	inicere, inieci, iniectus	*verb 3rd**	throw in
iactus	iacta, iactum	*(perfect passive participle of* iacio*)*	
iam	*indecl*	*adv*	now, already
ianua	ianuae	*noun f 1*	door
ibi	*indecl*	*adv*	there
idem	eadem, idem	*pron/adj*	the same
ieci		*(perfect of* iacio*)*	
iens	*gen* euntis	*(present participle of* eo*)*	
igitur	*indecl*	*conj*	therefore, and so
ii		*(=* ivi, *perfect of* eo*)*	
ille	illa, illud	*pron/adj*	that; he, she, it
imperator	imperatoris	*noun m 3*	general, leader; emperor
imperium	imperii	*noun n 2*	empire, power, command
impero	imperare, imperavi, imperatus	*verb 1st*	order, command (+ *dat*)
in	+ *acc/abl*	*prep*	(+ *acc*) into, onto; (+ *abl*) in, on
incendo	incendere, incendi, incensus	*verb 3rd*	burn, set on fire
infelix	*gen* infelicis	*adj*	unlucky, unhappy
ingens	*gen* ingentis	*adj*	huge
ingredior	ingredi, ingressus sum	*verb 3rd* dep*	enter
inicio	inicere, inieci, iniectus	*verb 3rd**	throw in
inimicus	inimici	*noun m 2*	enemy (*usu* personal)
inquit	*pl* inquiunt	*verb irreg*	(he) says, (he) said
insula	insulae	*noun f 1*	island; block of flats
intellego	intellegere, intellexi, intellectus	*verb 3rd*	understand, realise
inter	+ *acc*	*prep*	among, between

interea	*indecl*	*adv*	meanwhile
interficio	interficere, interfeci, interfectus	*verb 3rd**	kill
intro	intrare, intravi, intratus	*verb 1st*	enter
invenio	invenire, inveni, inventus	*verb 4th*	find
invito	invitare, invitavi, invitatus	*verb 1st*	invite
ipse	ipsa, ipsum	*pron*	self (*any person*), himself, herself, itself, *pl* selves, themselves
ira	irae	*noun f 1*	anger
iratus	irata, iratum	*adj*	angry
irrumpo	irrumpere, irrupi, irruptus	*verb 3rd*	burst in
is	ea, id	*pron*	he, she, it, *pl* they; that, *pl* those
ita	*indecl*	*adv*	in this way, to such an extent, so
itaque	*indecl*	*conj*	and so, therefore
iter	itineris	*noun n 3*	journey
iterum	*indecl*	*adv*	again
iubeo	iubere, iussi, iussus	*verb 2nd*	order
iussi		(*perfect of* iubeo)	
iussus	iussa, iussum	(*perfect passive participle of* iubeo)	
iuvenis	iuvenis	*noun m 3*	young man
ivi		(*perfect of* eo)	
labor	laboris	*noun m 3*	work
laboro	laborare, laboravi	*verb 1st*	work
lacrimo	lacrimare, lacrimavi	*verb 1st*	weep, cry
laetus	laeta, laetum	*adj*	happy
latus	lata, latum	(*perfect passive participle of* fero)	
laudo	laudare, laudavi, laudatus	*verb 1st*	praise
lectus	lecta, lectum	(*perfect passive participle of* lego)	
legio	legionis	*noun f 3*	legion
lego	legere, legi, lectus	*verb 3rd*	read; choose
lentus	lenta, lentum	*adj*	slow
leo	leonis	*noun m 3*	lion
libenter	*indecl*	*adv*	willingly, gladly
liber	libri	*noun m 2*	book
liberi	liberorum	*noun m 2 pl*	children
libero	liberare, liberavi, liberatus	*verb 1st*	set free
libertus	liberti	*noun m 2*	freedman, ex-slave
locus	loci (*pl is n:* loca)	*noun m/n 2*	place
locutus sum		(*perfect of* loquor)	
longus	longa, longum	*adj*	long
loquor	loqui, locutus sum	*verb 3rd dep*	speak
lux	lucis	*noun f 3*	light, daylight

magis	*indecl*	*adv*	more
magnopere	*indecl*	*adv*	greatly
magnus	magna, magnum	*adj*	big, large, great
maior	maius	*adj*	bigger, greater
maximus	maxima, maximum	*adj*	biggest, greatest, very big/great
malo	malle, malui	*verb irreg*	prefer
malus	mala, malum	*adj*	bad, evil
peior	peius	*adj*	worse
pessimus	pessima, pessimum	*adj*	worst, very bad
maneo	manere, mansi	*verb 2nd*	remain, stay
mansi		(*perfect of* maneo)	
manus	manus	*noun f 4*	hand; group of people
mare	maris	*noun n 3*	sea
maritus	mariti	*noun m 2*	husband
mater	matris	*noun f 3*	mother
maxime	*indecl*	*adv*	very greatly
maximus	maxima, maximum	*adj*	biggest, greatest, very big/great
medius	media, medium	*adj*	middle (of)
melior	melius	*adj*	better
mercator	mercatoris	*noun m 3*	merchant
meus	mea, meum	*adj*	my
miles	militis	*noun m 3*	soldier
mille	*pl* milia	*num*	1000
minime	*indecl*	*adv*	no; least, very little
minimus	minima, minimum	*adj*	very little, smallest
minor	minus	*adj*	smaller, less
miror	mirari, miratus sum	*verb 1st dep*	wonder at, admire
miser	misera, miserum	*adj*	miserable, wretched, sad
misi		(*perfect of* mitto)	
missus	missa, missum	(*perfect passive participle of* mitto)	
mitto	mittere, misi, missus	*verb 3rd*	send
modus	modi	*noun m 2*	manner, way, kind
moneo	monere, monui, monitus	*verb 2nd*	warn, advise
mons	montis	*noun m 3*	mountain
morior	mori, mortuus sum	*verb 3rd* dep*	die
mors	mortis	*noun f 3*	death
mortuus sum		(*perfect of* morior)	
motus	mota, motum	(*perfect passive participle of* moveo)	
moveo	movere, movi, motus	*verb 2nd*	move
mox	*indecl*	*adv*	soon
multus	multa, multum	*adj*	much, *pl* many
multo	*indecl*	*adv*	much, by much
plus	*gen* pluris	*adj*	more (of) (+ *gen*); *pl* more
plurimus	plurima, plurimum	*adj*	very much, *pl* very many, most
murus	muri	*noun m 2*	wall

nam	*indecl*	*conj*	for
narro	narrare, narravi, narratus	*verb 1st*	tell, relate
nauta	nautae	*noun m 1*	sailor
navigo	navigare, navigavi	*verb 1st*	sail
navis	navis	*noun f 3*	ship
-ne . . . ?	*indecl*	*adv*	(*makes open question, e.g.*) is it?
ne	*indecl*	*conj*	that . . . not, so that . . . not; (*after verb of fearing*) that, lest
nec/neque	*indecl*	*conj*	and not, nor, neither
nec . . . nec/neque . . . neque			neither . . . nor (*see page 157*)
neco	necare, necavi, necatus	*verb 1st*	kill
nemo	neminis	*irreg pron m/f*	no-one, nobody
nescio	nescire, nescivi	*verb 4th*	not know
nihil	*indecl*	*irreg pron n*	nothing
nisi	*indecl*	*conj*	unless, except
nolo	nolle, nolui	*verb irreg*	not want, refuse
nomen	nominis	*noun n 3*	name
non	*indecl*	*adv*	not
nonne?	*indecl*	*adv*	surely?
nonnulli	nonnullae, nonnulla	*adj*	some, several
nos	nostrum	*pron*	we, us
noster	nostra, nostrum	*adj*	our
novem	*indecl*	*num*	nine
novus	nova, novum	*adj*	new
nox	noctis	*noun f 3*	night
nullus	nulla, nullum	*adj*	not any, no . . .
num . . . ?	*indecl*	*adv*	surely . . . not?
num	*indecl*	*adv*	whether (*in indirect question*)
numquam	*indecl*	*adv*	never
nunc	*indecl*	*adv*	now
nuntio	nuntiare, nuntiavi, nuntiatus	*verb 1st*	announce
nuntius	nuntii	*noun m 2*	messenger, message, news
oblatus	oblata, oblatum	(*perfect passive participle of* offero)	
obtuli		(*perfect of* offero)	
occido	occidere, occidi, occisus	*verb 3rd*	kill
octo	*indecl*	*num*	eight
offero	offerre, obtuli, oblatus	*verb irreg*	offer
olim	*indecl*	*adv*	once, some time ago
omnis	omne	*adj*	all, every
opprimo	opprimere, oppressi, oppressus	*verb 3rd*	crush, overwhelm

oppugno	oppugnare, oppugnavi, oppugnatus	*verb 1st*	attack
optimus	optima, optimum	*adj*	best, excellent, very good
oro	orare, oravi, oratus	*verb 1st*	beg
ostendo	ostendere, ostendi, ostentus	*verb 3rd*	show
paene	*indecl*	*adv*	almost, nearly
paro	parare, paravi, paratus	*verb 1st*	prepare
pars	partis	*noun f 3*	part
parvus	parva, parvum	*adj*	small
minor	minus	*adj*	smaller, less
minimus	minima, minimum	*adj*	very little, smallest
passus sum		(*perfect of* patior)	
pater	patris	*noun m 3*	father
patior	pati, passus sum	*verb 3rd dep*	suffer, endure
patria	patriae	*noun f 1*	country, homeland
pauci	paucae, pauca	*adj pl*	few, a few
pax	pacis	*noun f 3*	peace
pecunia	pecuniae	*noun f 1*	money
peior	peius	*adj*	worse
pello	pellere, pepuli, pulsus	*verb 3rd*	drive
expello	expellere, expuli, expulsus	*verb 3rd*	drive out
repello	repellere, reppuli, repulsus	*verb 3rd*	drive back
per	+ *acc*	*prep*	through, along
pereo	perire, perii	*verb irreg*	die, perish
periculum	periculi	*noun n 2*	danger
persuadeo	persuadere, persuasi	*verb 2nd*	persuade (+ *dat*)
perterritus	perterrita, perterritum	*adj*	terrified
pervenio	pervenire, perveni	*verb 4th*	reach, arrive at
pes	pedis	*noun m 3*	foot
pessimus	pessima, pessimum	*adj*	worst, very bad
peto	petere, petivi, petitus	*verb 3rd*	seek, ask for, make for
plenus	plena, plenum	*adj*	full
plus	*gen* pluris	*adj*	more of (+ *gen*); *pl* more
plurimus	plurima, plurimum	*adj*	very much, *pl* very many, most
poena	poenae	*noun f 1*	punishment
poenas do			pay the penalty, be punished
pono	ponere, posui, positus	*verb 3rd*	place, put, put up
porta	portae	*noun f 1*	gate
porto	portare, portavi, portatus	*verb 1st*	carry
portus	portus	*noun m 4*	harbour, port

positus	posita, positum	(*perfect passive participle of* pono)	
possum	posse, potui	*verb irreg*	can, be able
post	+ *acc*	*prep*	after, behind
postea	*indecl*	*adv*	afterwards
postquam	*indecl*	*conj*	after, when
postridie	*indecl*	*adv*	on the next day
posui		(*perfect of* pono)	
potui		(*perfect of* possum)	
praemium	praemii	*noun n 2*	prize, reward, profit
precor	precari, precatus sum	*verb 1st dep*	pray (to), beg
primo	*indecl*	*adv*	at first
primus	prima, primum	*adj*	first
princeps	principis	*noun m 3*	chief; emperor
pro	+ *abl*	*prep*	in front of, for, in return for
procedo	procedere, processi	*verb 3rd*	advance, proceed
proelium	proelii	*noun n 2*	battle
proficiscor	proficisci, profectus sum	*verb 3rd dep*	set out
progredior	progredi, progressus sum	*verb 3rd dep*	advance
promitto	promittere, promisi, promissus	*verb 3rd*	promise
prope	+ *acc*	*prep*	near
propter	+ *acc*	*prep*	on account of, because of
proximus	proxima, proximum	*adj*	nearest, next to
puella	puellae	*noun f 1*	girl
puer	pueri	*noun m 2*	boy
pugno	pugnare, pugnavi	*verb 1st*	fight
pulcher	pulchra, pulchrum	*adj*	beautiful, handsome
punio	punire, punivi, punitus	*verb 4th*	punish
puto	putare, putavi, putatus	*verb 1st*	think
quaero	quaerere, quaesivi, quaesitus	*verb 3rd*	search for, look for, ask
qualis?	quale?	*adj*	what sort of?
quam (i)	*indecl*	*adv*	how ...! how ...?
quam celerrime (*or other sup adv*)			as (quickly) as possible
quam (ii)	*indecl*	*adv*	than
quamquam	*conj*		although
quando?	*indecl*	*adv*	when?
quantus?	quanta? quantum?	*adj*	how big? how much?
quattuor	*indecl*	*num*	four
-que	*indecl*	*conj*	and (*before word it is attached to*)
qui	quae, quod	*pron*	who, which
quidam	quaedam, quoddam	*pron*	a certain, one, some

quinque	*indecl*	*num*	five
quis?	quid?	*pron*	who? what?
quo?	*indecl*	*adv*	where to?
quod	*indecl*	*conj*	because
quomodo?	*indecl*	*adv*	how? in what way?
quoque	*indecl*	*conj*	also, too
quot?	*indecl*	*adj*	how many?
rapio	rapere, rapui, raptus	*verb 3rd**	seize, grab
re-	*indecl*	*prefix*	. . . back
reddo	reddere, reddidi, redditus	*verb 3rd*	give back, restore
redeo	redire, redii	*verb irreg*	go back, come back, return
refero	referre, rettuli, relatus	*verb irreg*	bring/carry back; report, tell
regina	reginae	*noun f 1*	queen
regnum	regni	*noun n 2*	kingdom
rego	regere, rexi, rectus	*verb 3rd*	rule, reign
regredior	regredi, regressus sum	*verb 3rd* dep*	go back, return
relinquo	relinquere, reliqui, relictus	*verb 3rd*	leave, leave behind
repello	repellere, reppuli, repulsus	*verb 3rd*	drive back
res	rei	*noun f 5*	thing, matter, event
resisto	resistere, restiti	*verb 3rd*	resist (+ *dat*)
respondeo	respondere, respondi, responsus	*verb 2nd*	reply
rex	regis	*noun m 3*	king
rideo	ridere, risi	*verb 2nd*	laugh, smile
risi		(*perfect of* rideo)	
rogo	rogare, rogavi, rogatus	*verb 1st*	ask, ask for
Roma	Romae (Romae = at/in Rome)	*noun f 1*	Rome
Romanus	Romana, Romanum	*adj*	Roman
rumpo	rumpere, rupi, ruptus	*verb 3rd*	burst, break
erumpo	erumpere, erupi, eruptus	*verb 3rd*	burst out
irrumpo	irrumpere, irrupi, irruptus	*verb 3rd*	burst in
sacer	sacra, sacrum	*adj*	sacred
saepe	*indecl*	*adv*	often
saevus	saeva, saevum	*adj*	savage, cruel
saluto	salutare, salutavi, salutatus	*verb 1st*	greet
salve!	*pl* salvete!	*imperat*	hello!
sanguis	sanguinis	*noun m 3*	blood
sapiens	*gen* sapientis	*adj*	wise
satis	*indecl*	*adv*	enough
scelestus	scelesta, scelestum	*adj*	wicked

scelus	sceleris	*noun n 3*	crime
scio	scire, scivi, scitus	*verb 4th*	know
scribo	scribere, scripsi, scriptus	*verb 3rd*	write
scripsi		*(perfect of* scribo*)*	
se	sui	*refl pron*	himself, herself, itself, themselves
secutus sum		*(perfect of* sequor*)*	
sed	*indecl*	*conj*	but
sedeo	sedere, sedi	*verb 2nd*	sit
semper	*indecl*	*adv*	always
senator	senatoris	*noun m 3*	senator
senex	senis	*noun m 3*	old man
sentio	sentire, sensi, sensus	*verb 4th*	feel, notice
septem	*indecl*	*num*	seven
sequor	sequi, secutus sum	*verb 3rd dep*	follow
servo	servare, servavi, servatus	*verb 1st*	save, keep, protect
servus	servi	*noun m 2*	slave
sex	*indecl*	*num*	six
si	*indecl*	*conj*	if
sic	*indecl*	*adv*	thus, in this way
signum	signi	*noun n 2*	sign, signal, standard
silva	silvae	*noun f 1*	wood
simul	*indecl*	*adv*	at the same time
simulac/ simulatque	*indecl*	*conj*	as soon as
sine	+ *abl*	*prep*	without
soleo	solere, solitus sum	*verb 2nd s-dep*	be accustomed
solus	sola, solum	*adj*	alone, on one's own, lonely, only
specto	spectare, spectavi, spectatus	*verb 1st*	look at, watch
spero	sperare, speravi, speratus	*verb 1st*	hope, expect
spes	spei	*noun f 5*	hope
statim	*indecl*	*adv*	at once, immediately
steti		*(perfect of* sto*)*	
sto	stare, steti	*verb 1st*	stand
stultus	stulta, stultum	*adj*	stupid, foolish
sub	+ *acc/abl*	*prep*	under, beneath
subito	*indecl*	*adv*	suddenly
sum	esse, fui	*verb irreg*	be
summus	summa, summum	*adj*	highest, greatest, top (of)
supero	superare, superavi, superatus	*verb 1st*	overcome, overpower
surgo	surgere, surrexi	*verb 3rd*	get up, stand up, rise
surrexi		*(perfect of* surgo*)*	
sustuli		*(perfect of* tollo*)*	

suus	sua, suum	*adj*	his, her, its, their (own) (*refl*)
taberna	tabernae	*noun f 1*	shop, inn
taceo	tacere, tacui	*verb 2nd*	be silent, be quiet
talis	tale	*adj*	such, of such a sort
tam	*indecl*	*adv*	so
tamen	*indecl*	*adv*	however
tandem	*indecl*	*adv*	at last, finally
tantus	tanta, tantum	*adj*	so great, such a great
tempestas	tempestatis	*noun f 3*	storm
templum	templi	*noun n 2*	temple
tempus	temporis	*noun n 3*	time
teneo	tenere, tenui, tentus	*verb 2nd*	hold
terra	terrae	*noun f 1*	earth, ground, land, country
terreo	terrere, terrui, territus	*verb 2nd*	frighten
timeo	timere, timui	*verb 2nd*	fear, be afraid
tollo	tollere, sustuli, sublatus	*verb 3rd*	raise, lift up, hold up
tot	*indecl*	*adj*	so many
totus	tota, totum	*adj*	whole
trado	tradere, tradidi, traditus	*verb 3rd*	hand over
traho	trahere, traxi, tractus	*verb 3rd*	drag
trans	+ *acc, or as prefix*	*prep*	across
traxi		(*perfect of* traho)	
tres	tria	*num*	three
tristis	triste	*adj*	sad
tu	tui	*pron*	you (*sg*)
tuli		(*perfect of* fero)	
tum	*indecl*	*adv*	then, at that time
turba	turbae	*noun f 1*	crowd
tuus	tua, tuum	*adj*	your (of you *sg*), yours
ubi	*indecl*	*adv*	(*question*) where? (*not question*) when, where
umquam	*indecl*	*adv*	ever
unde	*indecl*	*adv*	(*question*) where from? (*not question*) from where
unus	una, unum	*num*	one
urbs	urbis	*noun f 3*	city, town
ut	*indecl*	*conj*	(+ *subjunctive*) that, so that, in order to; (+ *indicative, or no verb*) as, when
uxor	uxoris	*noun f 3*	wife

vale	*pl* valete	*imperat*	goodbye! farewell!
validus	valida, validum	*adj*	strong
vehementer	*indecl*	*adv*	violently, loudly
vendo	vendere, vendidi, venditus	*verb 3rd*	sell
venio	venire, veni	*verb 4th*	come
verbum	verbi	*noun n 2*	word
verto	vertere, verti, versus	*verb 3rd*	turn
verus	vera, verum	*adj*	true, real
vester	vestra, vestrum	*adj*	your (of you *pl*), yours
via	viae	*noun f 1*	road, street, way
vici		(*perfect of* vinco)	
victoria	victoriae	*noun f 1*	victory
victus	victa, victum	(*perfect passive participle of* vinco)	
video	videre, vidi, visus	*verb 2nd*	see
videor	videri, visus sum	*verb 2nd dep*	seem, appear
villa	villae	*noun f 1*	house, country villa
vinco	vincere, vici, victus	*verb 3rd*	conquer, win, be victorious
vinum	vini	*noun n 2*	wine
vir	viri	*noun n 2*	man, male
virtus	virtutis	*noun f 3*	courage, virtue
visus	visa, visum	(*perfect passive participle of* video)	
vita	vitae	*noun f 1*	life
vivo	vivere, vixi	*verb 3rd*	live, be alive
vivus	viva, vivum	*adj*	alive, living
vixi		(*perfect of* vivo)	
voco	vocare, vocavi, vocatus	*verb 1st*	call
volo	velle, volui	*verb irreg*	want
vos	vestrum	*pron*	you (*pl*)
vox	vocis	*noun f 3*	voice, shout
vulnero	vulnerare, vulneravi, vulneratus	*verb 1st*	wound, injure
vulnus	vulneris	*noun n 3*	wound
vultus	vultus	*noun m 4*	expression, face

INDEX

ablative absolute 129–31
ablative case 10–11
accusative case 5–6
active and passive 91–2
adjectives 24–34
adverbs 35–9
agent 95
agreement of nouns and adjectives
    27–8

cases 1–11
characteristic vowels 71
comparative adjectives 29–30, 33–4
comparative adverbs 38–9
complement 2
complex sentences 159–61
compound verbs 64–5
conditional clauses 114–15
conjugations 68
conjunctions 66–7
connecting relative 116–17
cum clauses 152–3

dative case 9
declension and gender 12
declensions 13–23
defective verbs 90
deponent verbs 99–100
direct commands 102–3
direct questions 104–6
direct statement 132

endings xvi–xvii

first declension nouns 13–14
fourth and fifth declension nouns 22–3
future active participle 126–7
future passive 94
future tense 73

gender 12
genitive case 7–8
gerundive 142–3
grammar terms xii–xv

imperative 102
imperfect passive 93
imperfect subjunctive 138–41, 143–9,
    167
imperfect tense 71–2
indirect commands 144–5
indirect object 9
indirect questions 154–6
indirect statement 132–7
infinitives 74, 98, 133–4
instrument 95
irregular comparatives 33–4, 38–9
irregular perfect passive
        participles 123
irregular perfect tenses 80–1
irregular superlatives 33–4, 38–9
irregular verbs 75–6, 85–9

locative 63

negatives 157–8
nominative case 1–3
nouns 13–23
numerals 107–8

participles 118–28
passive 91–8, 139, 151
passive infinitive 98
perfect active participle 124–5
perfect passive 96–7
perfect passive participle 121–3
perfect tense 78–82
personal pronouns 41–4
pluperfect passive 96–7

pluperfect subjunctive 150–6
pluperfect tense 83–4
possessives 45–7
prefixes and compound verbs 64–5
prepositions 61–3
present active participle 118–20
present passive 93
present tense 70
principal parts 77
pronouns 40–60
purpose clauses 140–1

reflexive possessives 45–6
reflexive pronouns 42–3
relative pronoun and clauses 54–6
result clauses 146–8

second declension nouns 15–17
semi-deponent verbs 101
subjunctive 138–56, 167–8
superlative adjectives 31–4
superlative adverbs 38–9

third declension nouns 18–20
time clauses 111–12, 143
time expressions 109–10

verbs of fearing 149
vocative case 4

words easily confused 164–6
words with more than one
        meaning 162–3